STILL-LIFE PAINTING IN AMERICA

Messengers of Peace BY WILLIAM M. HARNETT

STILL-LIFE

PAINTING

IN

WOLFGANG BORN

AMERICA

OXFORD UNIVERSITY PRESS · New York · 1947

PRINTED IN THE UNITED STATES OF AMERICA

TO MY WIFE MARY

ACKNOWLEDGMENTS

IT IS *a pleasure to acknowledge the generous assistance I have received in preparing this volume. Numerous persons have aided me in gathering information and have given me the benefit of their advice. Miss Alice Winchester, editor of Antiques, encouraged me to undertake the study of American still-life painting. Dr. Siegfried Giedion, of the University of Zurich, Switzerland, and Dr. Heinrich Schwarz, of the Museum of Art, Providence, Rhode Island, have made available to me studies of theirs not yet published. Dr. Giedion has examined the effect of mechanization on modern civilization, and Dr. Schwarz has investigated the influence of mechanical devices, including the camera, on art.*

The Frick Art Reference Library in New York has generously allowed me to draw on its extensive sources of information; and other libraries, especially the New York Public Library, have made their facilities available in a most gratifying way. The owners of the pictures included here for purposes of illustration are named in the captions of the pictures. Without their kind permission to use these illustrations, this volume would have been impossible.

I am indebted to Louisiana State University for a grant made in support of the research and the preparation of materials that have gone into this book. My colleague, Professor Ralph Wickiser, has read the manuscript and has offered valuable suggestions.

I wish, further, to express my gratitude to others who contributed to my work as this study progressed: Mr. Jere Abbott, Director, the Smith College Museum, Northampton, Mass.; Mr. A. Everett Austin, Jr., Windham, N. H.; Mr. Charles E. Baker, Editor, the New York Historical Society; Mr. John J. H. Baur, Curator of Painting and Sculpture, The Brooklyn Museum; Mr. Alexander Bower, Director, L.D.M. Sweat Memorial Museum, Portland, Me.; Mr. Edmund Bury, *Philadelphia, Pa.; Miss Elizabeth Clare, N. Y.; Miss Nora E. Cordingley, Harvard College Library; Miss Bartlett Cowdrey, N. Y.; Mr. C. C. Cunningham, Director, Wadsworth Atheneum, Hartford, Conn.; Mrs. Fanny H. Eckstrom, Brewer, Me.; Miss Harriet R. Forbes, Orange Free Library, Orange, N. J.; Mr. James Thomas Flexner, Clintonville, Conn.; Miss Charlotte W. Hardy, Brewer, Mass.; Mr. Fiske Kimball, Director, Philadelphia Museum of Art; Mr. James W. Lane, National Gallery of Art, Washington, D. C.; Mrs. Jean Lipman, Editor, Art in America; Miss Marion Lawrence, Library Association of Portland, Portland, Ore.; Mrs. Margaret S. Lundy, Williamsport, Pa.; Miss Pearl A. Madden, Orange, N. J.; Mr. Frank Jewett Mather, Director, Museum of Historic Art, Princeton, N. J.; Mr. Jeremiah O'Connor, Curator, The Corcoran Gallery of Art, Washington; Mr. John O'Connor, Jr., Assistant Director, Carnegie Institute, Pittsburgh, Pa.; Mrs. Barbara N. Parker, Curator of Paintings, Museum of Fine Arts, Boston, Mass.; Dr. J. Hall Pleasants, Baltimore, Md.; Mrs. Barbara S. Roberts, Pennsylvania Academy of the Fine Arts, Philadelphia, Pa.; Mr. Frederick B. Robinson, Director, Museum of Fine Arts, Springfield, Mass.; Mr. Edgar Preston Richardson, Director, the Detroit Institute of Art; Mr. Charles Coleman Sellers, Wesleyan University, Middletown, Conn.; Mr. Donald A. Shelley, Curator of Painting and Sculpture, the New York Historical Society; Mrs. Fern Shapley, National Gallery of Art, Washington, D. C.; Mr. Charles Sterling, The Metropolitan Museum of Art; Dr. Helmut P. Seckel, Chicago, Ill.; Mr. R. P. Tolman, Acting Director, National Collection of Fine Arts, Washington; Mr. Karl G. Weston, Director, Williams College, Williamstown, Mass.; Miss Virginia Yarbro, Ryerson Library, Chicago.*

TABLE OF CONTENTS

LIST OF ILLUSTRATIONS

*All measurements are given in inches. When it has been impossible
to determine the date of the picture, the artist's life-dates are given.*

Frontispiece: William M. Harnett, *Messengers of Peace*, oil on canvas, 27½ by 33¾, 1890, sgd., courtesy of the Springfield Museum of Fine Arts, Springfield, Mass. Color plate courtesy of *Life* magazine.

1. Jacopo de Barbari, *Dead Partridge*, oil on panel, 19⅒ by 16⅖, 1504, sgd., Alte Pinakothek, Munich. Photo courtesy of the Metropolitan Museum of Art, New York.

2. Melchior de Hondecoeter (1636-95), *The Dead Cock*, oil on canvas, 43³⁄₁₀ by 32⅖, sgd., Musées Royaux des Beaux-Arts, Brussels. Photo courtesy of the Metropolitan Museum of Art, New York.

3. Wallerant Vaillant, *Letter Rack*, oil on canvas, 20 by 15⁷⁄₁₀, 1658, sgd., Staatliche Museen, Dresden. Photo courtesy of the Metropolitan Museum of Art, New York.

4. Samuel van Hoogstraten, *Perspective Box of a Dutch Interior with Still Life*, walnut box: h. 16½, w. 12½ & 11¼, 1663, sgd., courtesy of the Detroit Institute of Arts, Detroit.

5. Otto Marsaeus van Schrieck, *Close-up of Underbrush with Animals*, oil on canvas, 39¼ by 29½, 1667, sgd., courtesy of the New-York Historical Society, New York.

6. Jean-Baptiste Oudry (1685-1755), *Library*, oil on canvas, 24 by 30, courtesy of Arnold Seligmann, Rey & Co., New York.

7. Appolinar Fonseca, *Still Life*, oil on canvas, 28 by 38, 1852, sgd., collection of Mr. Roberto Montenegro, Mexico City. Photo courtesy of the Museum of Modern Art, New York.

8. Francisco de Zurbarán, *Still Life*, oil on canvas, 24½ by 51, c. 1633, courtesy of the City Art Museum, St. Louis, Mo.

9. Caravaggio (1569-1609), *Still Life*, oil on canvas, 19⅞ by 28¼, courtesy of the National Gallery of Art, Washington, D. C. (Kress Collection).

10. Jean-Baptiste Siméon Chardin, *Kitchen Still Life*, oil on canvas, 1764, sgd., 38 by 60, courtesy of M. Knoedler & Co., New York.

11. Cornelius van Spaendonck, *Flowers*, oil on canvas, 12½ by 15½, 1829, sgd., courtesy of M. Knoedler & Co., New York.

12. Franz Xaver Petter, *Still Life, Fruit and Flowers*, oil on panel, 14¼ by 17½, 1822, sgd., courtesy of Mr. Louis Lion, New York.

13. Carl Schuch (1846-1903), *Still Life*, oil on canvas, 26 by 32, sgd., courtesy of Mr. Louis Lion, New York.

14. Charles Willson Peale, *Fruit Bowl*, **Detail of Family Group**, oil on canvas, 56½ by 89½, 1773-1809, sgd., courtesy of the New-York Historical Society, New York.

15. James Peale, *Fruits of Autumn*, oil on canvas, 15½ by 22, probably before 1820, courtesy of the Whitney Museum of American Art, New York.

16. James Peale, *Still Life, Fruit*, oil on panel, 18½ by 26½, 1825, sgd., courtesy of the Worcester Art Museum, Worcester, Mass.

17. James Peale, *Still Life, Fruit*, oil on canvas, 20 by 26½, 1827, sgd., courtesy of the Pennsylvania Academy of Fine Arts, Philadelphia.

18. James Peale, *Still Life, Watermelon and Grapes*, 18¼ by 26, 1824, sgd., courtesy of the Wadsworth Atheneum, Hartford, Conn.

19. Raphaelle Peale, *Apples and Fox Grapes*, oil on panel, 11½ by 13, 1815, sgd., courtesy of the Pennsylvania Academy of Fine Arts, Philadelphia.

20. Raphaelle Peale, *Still Life with a Glass, Plate, Biscuit and Fruit*, oil on panel, 10¼ by 13⅝, 1818, sgd., courtesy of the Detroit Institute of Arts, Detroit.

21. Raphaelle Peale, *Still Life with Peaches*, oil on panel, 13¼ by 19¼, 1821, sgd., courtesy of the Brooklyn Museum, Brooklyn, N. Y.

22. Raphaelle Peale, *Still Life with Watermelon*, oil on canvas, 24 by 29, 1822, sgd., courtesy of the Springfield Museum of Fine Arts, Springfield, Mass. (James Philip Gray Collection).

23. Raphaelle Peale, *Still Life with Wild Strawberries*, oil on canvas, 16 by 22, 1822, sgd., courtesy of James Graham & Co., New York.

24. Raphaelle Peale, *Still Life, Liqueur and Fruit*, oil on canvas, 13¼ by 19¾, probably 1822, sgd., courtesy of the Whitney Museum of American Art, New York.

25. Raphaelle Peale, *Still Life with Vegetables*, oil on panel, 11 by 14½, c. 1823, courtesy of the Wadsworth Atheneum, Hartford, Conn.

26. Raphaelle Peale, *Still Life, Melons*, oil on canvas, 19 by 23, c. 1823, sgd., courtesy of James Graham & Co., New York.

27. Robert Street, *Fruit in Basket*, oil on panel, 10¼ by 13¾, 1818, sgd., courtesy of Mr. Paul Lane, New York.

28. Raphaelle Peale, *After the Bath*, oil on canvas, 28 by 23, 1823, sgd., courtesy of the William Rockhill Nelson Gallery of Art, Kansas City, Mo.

29. Sarah Peale (1800-1885), *Peaches*, oil on canvas, 22 by 18, courtesy of the Ferargil Galleries, New York.

30. Attributed to James Peale (1749-1831), *Still Life with Fruit in a Bowl*, oil on canvas, 20 by 27, courtesy of the Museum of Fine Arts, Boston.

31. Artist unknown, *Still Life*, oil on canvas, 9¾ by 13, c. 1835, courtesy of Mr. A. F. Mondschein, New York.

32. Rubens Peale, *Flower Piece*, oil on canvas, 20 by 24, 1856, sgd., Andrew Weisenberg, Langhorne, Pa. Photo courtesy of the Frick Art Reference Library, New York.

33. Rubens Peale, *Two Grouse in Underbrush of Laurel*, oil on canvas, 19½ by 27, 1864, sgd., courtesy of the Detroit Institute of Arts, Detroit.

34. Rubens Peale, *The American Dessert*, oil on canvas, 19¼ by 27, probably c. 1860, sgd., courtesy of Mr. Theodore F. Bernstein, New York.

35. Abraham Woodside, *Bowl with Apples*, oil on panel, 12 by 17, 1839, sgd., courtesy of Rudolph Heinemann, New York.

36. Margaretta Angelica Peale (1795-1882), *Strawberries and Cherries*, oil on canvas, 10 by 12½, courtesy of the Pennsylvania Academy of Fine Arts, Philadelphia.

37. George Cope, *Still Life with Apples and Watermelons*, oil on canvas, 20 by 26, 1913, sgd., courtesy of Mr. Harry Stone, New York.

38. Mary Jane Peale, *Spring Flowers in Vase*, oil on canvas, 12 by 18, 1858, sgd., courtesy of Mr. Harry Stone, New York.

39. Pennsylvania German Folk Art, *Stylized Flowers*, water color on paper, 7¾ by 5, c. 1800, courtesy of the American Folk Art Collection, Williamsburg, Va.

40. Artist unknown, *Assorted Fruit*, water color on paper, 25¾ by 16, found in New York State, c. 1830, courtesy of the Downtown Gallery, New York.

41. Chipman, *Still Life with Melons and Grapes*, oil on canvas, 20 by 23¾, c. 1840, sgd., courtesy of the Harry Shaw Newman Gallery, New York.

42. Adèle Evans, *Basket of Flowers and Fruit*, panel, 22½ by 29½, c. 1835, sgd., courtesy of the Harry Shaw Newman Gallery, New York.

43. Artist unknown, *Still Life with Singing Bird*, pastel on paper, 22 by 18, c. 1800, courtesy of Mr. Harry Stone, New York.

44. Amory L. Babcock, *Flower Basket and Fruits*, water color on paper, 29 by 23, 1857, sgd. Ownership unknown, photo courtesy of the Harry Shaw Newman Gallery, New York.

45. Artist unknown, *Flowers on Black Marble Table*, water color on paper, 21 by 18, c. 1835, courtesy of Mr. Harry Stone, New York.

46. Artist unknown, *Blue Urn with Peonies and Roses*, velvet painting, 17¼ by 19½, c. 1820, collection of Mr. R. Allerton, Chicago. Photo courtesy of the Downtown Gallery, New York.

47. Thomas Sully, *Mrs. Boyd and Mrs. Smith*, oil on canvas, 34½ by 44¼, 1823, sgd., courtesy of M. Knoedler & Co., New York.

48. Artist unknown, *Fruit*, water color on paper, 12 by 14½, c. 1820, courtesy of the Museum of Art, Rhode Island School of Design, Providence, R. I.

49. Mary Vincent, *Tipped Bowl*, painting on velvet, 23 by 18, c. 1830, sgd., courtesy of the Downtown Gallery, New York.

50. Artist unknown, *Basket of Fruit*, painting on velvet, 14½ by 13, c. 1820, courtesy of the Museum of Art, Rhode Island School of Design, Providence, R. I.

51. Artist unknown, *Basket of Fruit*, painting on velvet, 16½ by 20½, c. 1820, courtesy of the Museum of Art, Rhode Island School of Design, Providence, R. I.

52. William S. Mount, *Spring Bouquet*, oil on paper, 7 by 6¾, 1859, sgd., Miss Anne O. Price, Glenn Cove, Long Island, New York. Photo courtesy of the Brooklyn Museum, Brooklyn, N. Y.

53. Joseph Biays Ord, *Déjeuner à la Fourchette*, oil on canvas, 13 by 19¼, 1840, sgd., courtesy of Mr. Bernard H. Cone, New York.

54. John F. Francis, *Grapes in a Dish*, oil on canvas, 25 by 30, c. 1850, courtesy of Mr. Prew Savoy, Washington, D. C.

55. John F. Francis, *Cheese, Chestnuts, and Crackers*, oil on canvas, 18 by 24, c. 1850, courtesy of the Ferargil Galleries, New York.

56. John F. Francis, *Apples in a Basket*, oil on canvas, 25 by 30, 1854, sgd., courtesy of Mr. Prew Savoy, Washington, D. C.

57. John F. Francis, *Still Life with Biscuit*, oil on canvas, 11 by 14, 1866, sgd., courtesy of the Museum of Historic Art, Princeton University, Princeton, N. J.

58. John F. Francis, *Still Life with Upturned Cherry Basket*, oil on canvas, 10¾ by 13¾, 1866, sgd., ownership unknown.

59. John F. Francis, *Still Life with Raisins and Oranges*, oil on canvas, 10½ by 13¼, 1866, sgd., ownership unknown.

60. John F. Francis, *Still Life*, oil on canvas, 25 by 30, c. 1870, sgd., courtesy of the Harry Shaw Newman Gallery, New York.

61. J. P. Hardy, *Three Pears between Grapes*, oil on canvas, 12 by 14, probably 1850-60, courtesy of Miss Charlotte Hardy, Brewer, Maine.

62. Severin Roesen, *Nature's Bounty*, oil on canvas, 34 by 50, 1860-70, sgd., courtesy of Mrs. Juliana Force, New York.

63. Severin Roesen, *Flowers*, oil on canvas, 50 by 36, c. 1867, sgd., Van Wyck Hall, Fishkill, N. Y. Photo courtesy of the Frick Art Reference Library, New York.

64. Severin Roesen, *Fruits*, oil on canvas, 50 by 36, c. 1867, sgd., Van Wyck Hall, Fishkill, N. Y. Photo courtesy of the Frick Art Reference Library, New York.

65. James Welles Champney, *The Wedding Gifts*, oil on canvas, 28 by 35, c. 1880, sgd., courtesy of Mrs. Alice G. B. Lockwood, Greenwich, Conn.

66. George H. Hall, *Holly*, oil on canvas, 15½ by 24⅛, 1871, sgd., courtesy of the Harry Shaw Newman Gallery, New York.

67. Nathaniel Peck, *The All-Seeing Eye*, oil on panel, 22½ by 19, 1827, sgd., courtesy of the Wadsworth Atheneum, Hartford, Conn.

68. F. Danton, Jr., *Time Is Money*, oil on canvas, 17 by 21, 1894, sgd., courtesy of the Wadsworth Atheneum, Hartford, Conn.

69. Charles Bird King, *Vanity of an Artist's Dream*, oil on canvas, 53¼ by 29½, 1830, sgd., courtesy of the Fogg Museum of Art, Harvard University, Cambridge, Mass.

70. Goldsborough Bruff, *Assorted Prints*, water color on paper, 11 by 14, c. 1845, sgd., courtesy of the Downtown Gallery, New York.

71. Martin J. Heade, *Flower Still Life*, oil on canvas, 17½ by 13¾, c. 1880, sgd., courtesy of Mr. A. F. Mondschein, New York.

72. Martin J. Heade, *Orchids and Hummingbird*, oil on canvas, 14 by 22, c. 1865, sgd., courtesy of the Macbeth Gallery, New York.

73. Martin J. Heade, *Gremlin in the Studio*, oil on canvas, 14 by 10, c. 1890, sgd., courtesy of Mr. Edwin Hewitt, New York.

74. Morston Constantine Ream, *Still Life*, oil on cardboard, 8 by 6, 1871, sgd., courtesy of the Springfield Museum of Fine Arts, Springfield, Mass.

75. Artist unknown, *Locomotive Entering Yard at Night*, oil on canvas, 7¾ by 17½, c. 1880, courtesy of Mr. John Jacob Astor, New York.

76. William M. Harnett, *To the Opera*, oil on canvas, 7 by 9, 1870, sgd., courtesy of the Downtown Gallery, New York.

77. William M. Harnett, *Raspberries and Ice Cream*, oil on canvas, 12 by 10, sgd., 1870, courtesy of the Ferargil Galleries, New York.

78. William M. Harnett, *Writing Table*, oil on canvas, 8 by 12, 1877, sgd., courtesy of the Philadelphia Museum of Art, Philadelphia.

79. William M. Harnett, *Basket of Catawba Grapes*, oil on canvas, 27½ by 22, 1876, sgd., collection of Mr. M. A. Chase, Cincinnati. Photo courtesy of the Downtown Gallery, New York.

80. William M. Harnett, *Just Dessert*, oil on canvas, 26½ by 22¼, 1891, sgd., courtesy of the Art Institute of Chicago, Chicago.

81. William M. Harnett, *Still Life with New York Ledger*, oil on canvas, 9¾ by 14, 1880, sgd., courtesy of Mr. Robert Freund, New York.

82. William M. Harnett, *Fruit Piece*, oil on canvas, 12 by 14, 1877, sgd., courtesy of the Downtown Gallery, New York.

83. William M. Harnett, *To Edwin Booth*, oil on panel, 15 by 19, 1879, sgd., courtesy of the Downtown Gallery, New York.

84. William M. Harnett, *The Faithful Colt*, oil on canvas, 22½ by 19, 1890, sgd., courtesy of the Wadsworth Atheneum, Hartford, Conn.

85. William M. Harnett, *Old Souvenirs*, oil on canvas, 26½ by 21½, 1881, sgd., courtesy of Mr. Oliver Jennings, New York.

86. William M. Harnett, *For Sunday Dinner*, oil on canvas, 40 by 52, 1884, sgd., courtesy of the Downtown Gallery, New York.

87. William M. Harnett, *The Trophy of the Hunt*, oil on canvas, 22 by 42½, 1885, sgd., courtesy of the Carnegie Institute, Pittsburgh.

88. William M. Harnett, *Mandolin*, oil on canvas, 25 by 30, 1890, sgd., collection of Miss Jania Whitman. Photo courtesy of the Ferargil Galleries, New York.

89. William M. Harnett, *The Old Cupboard Door*, oil on canvas, 54 by 28, 1892, sgd., courtesy of the Museum of Fine Arts, Boston.

90. William M. Harnett, *Discarded Treasures*, oil on canvas, 20⅛ by 40, c. 1889, sgd., courtesy of the Smith College Museum of Art, Northampton, Mass.

91. William M. Harnett, *Ten-Cent Bill*, oil on panel, 5½ by 7½, 1879, courtesy of the Philadelphia Museum of Art, Philadelphia.

92. W. S. Reynolds, *Time, Religion and Politics*, oil on canvas, 18 by 14, 1894, sgd., courtesy of M. Knoedler & Co., New York.

93. J. Haberle, *Twenty-Dollar Bill*, oil on canvas, 7½ by 9½, 1890, sgd., courtesy of the Springfield Museum of Fine Arts, Springfield, Mass.

94. J. Haberle, *Cigar Box and Pipe*, oil on canvas, 12½ by 11½, c. 1890, sgd., courtesy of the Springfield Museum of Fine Arts, Springfield, Mass.

95. John F. Peto, *Memories of 1865*, oil on canvas, 30 by 22, 1879, sgd., courtesy of the Wadsworth Atheneum, Hartford, Conn.

96. Richard LaBarre Goodwin, *Theodore Roosevelt's Cabin Door*, oil on canvas, 81¼ by 42, 1905-10, sgd., courtesy of the Springfield Museum of Fine Arts, Springfield, Mass.

97. Edmund E. Case (c. 1840-1919), *Woodcock*, oil on canvas, 18 by 15, sgd., courtesy of the Springfield Museum of Fine Arts, Springfield, Mass.

98. Alexander Pope (1829-1924), *Quail*, oil on canvas, 15 by 18, sgd., courtesy of M. Knoedler & Co., New York.

99. Frances Palmer (Bond), *Landscape, Fruit and Flowers*, color lithograph, 19¾ by 27½, 1863, sgd., courtesy of Harry Shaw Newman, Old Print Shop, New York.

100. A. J. H. Way (1826-1883), *Apples*, oil on canvas, 22 by 30, sgd., courtesy of the Peabody Institute, Baltimore, Md.

101. Edwards Bowers, *Still Life with Flagon and Fruits*, oil on canvas, 20 by 16, 1865, sgd., courtesy of Mr. A. F. Mondschein, New York.

102. Ralph Albert Blakelock (1847-1919), *Flower Piece*, oil on panel, 11½ by 7¾, sgd., courtesy of Mr. Paul Lane, New York.

103. Worthington Whittredge, *Laurel Blossoms in a Blue Vase*, water color, 15½ by 11, c. 1880, sgd., courtesy of Mr. and Mrs. Edward Kesler, Philadelphia.

104. Artist unknown, *Hollyhocks*, oil on canvas, 10¼ by 12, c. 1880, courtesy of M. Knoedler & Co., New York.

105. Frank Duveneck, *Still Life with Watermelon*, oil on canvas, 25 by 38⅛, c. 1878, sgd., courtesy of the Cincinnati Museum of Art, Cincinnati.

106. John La Farge, *Calla Lily*, oil on panel, 15½ by 9, 1862, sgd., courtesy of Prof. Frank Jewett Mather, Jr., Princeton, N. J.

107. John La Farge, *Magnolia Grandiflora*, oil on panel, 35 by 17, c. 1860, sgd., courtesy of the Lawrence Art Museum, Williamstown, Mass.

108. John La Farge, *Hollyhocks and Corn*, oil on panel, 23½ by 16½, 1865, sgd., courtesy of the Museum of Fine Arts, Boston.

109. John La Farge, *Vase of Flowers*, oil on panel, 18½ by 14, 1864, sgd., courtesy of the Museum of Fine Arts, Boston.

110. John La Farge, *Wreath*, oil on canvas, 23¼ by 12⅝, 1866, sgd., courtesy of the National Collection of Fine Arts, Smithsonian Institution, Washington, D. C.

111. William Merritt Chase (1849-1916), *An English Cod*, oil on canvas, 36 by 40, sgd., courtesy of the Corcoran Gallery of Art, Washington, D. C.

112. William Merritt Chase (1849-1916), *Still Life with Fish*, oil on canvas, 23 by 32, sgd., courtesy of the Pennsylvania Academy of Fine Arts, Philadelphia.

113. Emil Carlsen (1853-1932), *The White Jug*, oil on panel, 21¾ by 26¾, sgd., courtesy of the Corcoran Gallery of Art, Washington, D. C.

STILL-LIFE PAINTING IN AMERICA

STATING THE PROBLEM

STILL LIFE is the chamber music of painting: a singularly pure and refined form of artistic expression. It manifests the intrinsic values of art, very little diluted by incidental elements. For that reason the study of still life is no less rewarding as an aesthetic experience than as an historical discipline.

If this observation holds true for still life in general, it has special significance for American still life. American painting developed during one of the most confused periods in the history of art. Since the beginning of the twentieth century, this confusion has been fully analyzed with the result that most of the evaluations previously accepted have been gradually revised. It has been recognized that under a surface layer of pretentious academic art there existed strata of unassuming but genuine art production. American still life, all but forgotten by art historians until the present century, is such a stratum.

To be sure, American still life is a humble annex to the art of the world. But since civilization is indivisible, each single contribution to it is related to all others; and principles valid for monuments of universal significance are also valid for modest, regional undercurrents. Consequently for a study such as this, a suitable terminology must be devised to link these undercurrents to the great movements in the history of art—a terminology flexible enough to meet the requirements of the specific subject. Such terms are introduced and defined as needed.

The task of writing the history of an undercurrent —and that is what still-life painting in America is— conditions the approach of the author to his subject. The materials must be analyzed and grouped so as to allow a clear distinction of trends. The closer these trends are to the substrata of all art, the more universal their character will be, for underlying any development are what Strzygowski called 'the forces of gravity': the 'constants' of geography and climate, and the elements of tradition embodied in the crafts. Yet, the historian must realize that as a rule the work of the highly trained artist will follow the evolution of styles as revealed in the advanced production at the leading art centers of the world.

The objective of this book is to interpret a development that has been neglected previously, but that contains unmistakable creative values. Because new movements in art elude detached judgment by contemporaries, and because of the many ramifications of contemporary productions, this study of the history of still-life painting in America ends with the analysis of an older movement, surviving even now, in which a distinctly American idiom matured into a style of universal validity.

The author has not tried to make this an exhaustive study of the entire corpus of American still-life painting; much regional research must be done before such an objective can be accomplished. If this book succeeds in stimulating further research in its field, it will fulfil his sincere hope.

For the sake of continuity in presentation, biographical notes, references, and amplifications have been held to a minimum. Supplementary notes of such a nature have been assembled in an appendix, where each note is preceded by the page and line numbers of the corresponding passage in the text.

I. SOURCES AND PARALLELS

THE EARLIEST example of still-life painting known to us in the art of Europe is by Hans Memling: a bunch of wild flowers in a majolica pitcher placed on a table. The table is covered with an oriental rug of geometric design, and the whole is seen in a strictly frontal view. No accessories divert attention from the main motif. It is a painter's painting, quite unique in its period—the late fifteenth century—and Memling evidently did it for himself, for it is on the back of a portrait. Earlier in the century the Van Eycks had developed a naturalism that included still-life effects, but the still-life motifs were subordinated to the function of the picture, which was either a portrait or a religious representation. When Memling painted his bunch of flowers, he set a precedent, not only in type but also in style. The rigidly frontal composition, the concentration on a purely representational problem, and the precision of the treatment produce an effect which can be best characterized by the term 'objectivism.'

Objectivism aims at the detached illustration of an object. This springs from an interest in the thing itself. Since the relation of the object to its surroundings tends to confuse the eye, an objectivist painter isolates it as much as possible. The subject of a truly objectivist painting takes on the semblance of something absolute.

Memling also applied the principle demonstrated in his flower piece in a 'Vanitas' still life, the first example of its kind known to us. It pictures a human skull in a niche. On the wall below the sill of the niche is an inscription of the *memento mori* type. The skull is seen objectively isolated by the niche, and its volume is emphasized by precise modeling.

It is not accidental that Memling's still lifes date from a time when the principles of the Italian Renaissance were beginning to spread to the north, for a representation of reality presupposes a familiarity with perspective, and the laws of perspective were developed during the Renaissance.

Albrecht Dürer, who heralded the victory of the Renaissance in Germany, applied to close-ups of plants the same principle as that found earlier in Memling's *Flowers*. He isolated 'foreground motifs' and thus created a new subject in modern Western art. Although in the strictest sense a landscape, the close-up is so near the still life in spirit that it is by general consent considered as such.

In an endeavor to depict reality as convincingly as possible, the Renaissance developed the peep show. This optical toy was invented by the architect Leon Battista Alberti, who contributed to the development of perspective. The peep show is a box with a magnifying lens on one side and a lighted picture on the other. Figures and other properties are often placed in tiers before the backdrop. Viewed through the lens, their image appears in relief, enlarged and sharpened, or 'super-real' (fig. 4). If objects in a painting are depicted on a single plane or in tiers parallel to the picture plane, and if each part is painted with extreme attention to detail and texture, a similar effect is achieved. The French call this type of painting *trompe l'œil*, because it 'deceives the eye.'

The *Dead Partridge* by Jacopo de' Barbari, Dürer's teacher in perspective, is the earliest known example of *trompe l'œil* (fig. 1). It was painted in 1504. The partridge, together with the bolt of a crossbow and a pair of gauntlets, is suspended from a hook in a wall that extends across the picture. A slip of paper, casually attached to the wall, bears the signature of the artist. Jacopo de' Barbari's painting differs from the still life of Memling in its studied informality—it has nothing to set the painted objects apart from the rest of the world as the niche in the painting by Memling; on the contrary, it makes us forget we are looking at a painting.

The illusion is strong, but the painting does not actually approximate reality, for only a stereoscopic view gives a truly three-dimensional illusion. Rather it gives the effect of reality intensified or heightened. The *trompe l'œil* captures in painting the effect of the peep show.

A glance into a stereoscope shows us the world as we are accustomed to see it. A *trompe l'œil*, however, always produces weird effects because the painter has heightened the realism of his objects. Furthermore, this effect is increased because the painter is limited to the arrangement of objects in planes or tiers. Only by reducing the depth of his picture space to the very minimum can the painter hope to 'deceive the eye' in regard to the three-dimensionality of what it perceives. Hence the subject matter is also necessarily limited. The *trompe l'œil* must, even more than other types of painting, rely on the co-operation of the spectator.

An especially weird *trompe l'œil* can be achieved by the artist through combining heterogeneous objects. Pictured in the same plane or in parallel planes, and represented super-realistically, they give the impression that a transcendental bond exists between them and they are charged with a mysterious significance.

The still lifes by Memling, Dürer, and Jacopo de' Barbari represent three types that did not become popular until much later. Still lifes appeared rarely during the sixteenth century, for before the Baroque period, interest in an art without religious, literary, or historical appeal was not sufficient to stimulate a sizable growth of still-life painting.

The Baroque, in contradistinction to the linear and sculptural qualities of Renaissance art, pictured the world as an interplay of light and shadow, of tone and color. At the end of the sixteenth century, Caravaggio, master of the 'cellar light' effects, or, as the Italians call it, *tenebroso*, developed the 'picturesque' still life, typical of the Baroque (fig. 9). The 'picturesque' still life spread rapidly, and in its wake the 'objectivist,' and what is here termed the 'illusionist' still life developed beyond the stage of isolated and sporadic ventures.

Holland and Spain became the most important centers of still-life painting during the seventeenth century. In both countries the *tenebroso* manner of Caravaggio became the starting point of an evolution that was to produce highly dissimilar results. Rembrandt idealized the *tenebroso* as a mystic language of light, and the Dutch 'little masters' subsequently mellowed his spiritual idiom into a convenient device for rendering their prosaic subject matter more poetic. Schools of fruit and flower painters and painters of kitchen still lifes flourished. The de Heems, a dynasty of still-life painters, the best of whom was Jan, had done the lion's share in establishing the 'canonic' form of the Dutch fruit piece: a gorgeous array of luscious grapes, pears, and half-peeled lemons distributed on a table between precious glass and silverware. Draped napkins alternate with velvets and oriental rugs. Flower painting culminated in the work of Jan van Huysum, who lived until the middle of the eighteenth century. Van Huysum specialized in highly decorative arrangements of roses, tulips, and other garden flowers that form an intricate, softly glowing pattern in front of a dark background. His contemporary Rachel Ruych was the first of a series of women painters who carried the Van Huysum type of flower painting far into the nineteenth century. The others were, in chronological order (together with one man): Margareta Haverman, Jan van Os, Margareta van Os, and Maria Vos of Oosterbeek. In the hands of his followers, Van Huysum's delicate color and draftsmanship gradually gave way to a cold and more conventional treatment.

The kitchen still life rarely lost its connection with its matrix, *genre* painting. It became a really independent art form only when it was refined into the 'breakfast piece' by Pieter Claesz, the two Hedas, and other masters of the Haarlem School of the seventeenth century. Whether by means of a sober and plain arrangement of herring, bread, and beer, in cheap pottery and glassware; or through the display of fashionable silver pitchers, golden goblets, and Chinese porcelain filled with all kinds of delicacies, the artist catered to a cultivated well-to-do merchant class. Art to them became equivalent to sensuous delight.

In Spain during the first half of the seventeenth century, Velasquez subdued the *tenebroso* and raised realism to the level of a sublime aesthetic experience. His own kitchen pieces, works of his youth, included human figures, and thus were not true still lifes. But the painters of *bodegones* (studio pieces), who were influenced by him, disassociated themselves from figure painting completely. Their still lifes are forceful and massive. They belong to the world of the market, of the popular inn, of the farm.

Both in Spain and in Holland, undercurrents of illusionism made themselves felt, but in most instances they were blended with elements of the picturesque still life. The popular motif of the *memento mori* stimulated the development of the 'Vanitas' still lifes, which, after the model of Memling, were arranged with a skull as their central theme.

The new vogue of illusionism paralleled a peculiar intellectual curiosity, which centered in strange and rare things. During the late Renaissance the first steps were taken toward the establishment of the modern museum. The first stage was the curio cabinet, in which were included natural history, works of art, and all kinds of odd things that appealed to the collectors—most of whom were princes, merchants, or influential scholars. From the late sixteenth to the early eighteenth century, curio cabinets were established all over Europe. They supplied an answer to a widespread, passionate interest in the unknown, one barely satisfied by the natural sciences, then in their infancy, and one that was largely responsible for the upsurge of astrology, alchemy, and magic—esoteric doctrines that flourished during the Baroque period. All these branches of occultism agreed in attributing a mysterious life to dead matter. Not only was an object considered to be what it represents to the scientific mind, but, under favorable circumstances, it could have supernatural properties like those attributed by primitive man to his fetish. This is the background of the belief in amulets, which during this period was raised to the level of a highly complex, pseudoscientific theory. The so-called 'doctrine of signatures' was likewise an essential part of this system of thought—a doctrine according to which a natural object through an accidental similarity to a diseased human organ could become the bearer of a magic healing power. Some of the gallery interiors of the seventeenth century show in the homes of famous collectors, grotesquely shaped stones and shells, stuffed exotic birds and fishes, horns of foreign animals and other rarities spread out among fine paintings, antique sculptures, and masterpieces of the minor arts.

Among its varied showpieces a well-furnished curio cabinet also contained mechanical instruments, particularly optical instruments, which more often than not were like toys. They included automata and peep shows, or even combinations of both. Peep shows enjoyed a great popularity during the Baroque, for they epitomized illusionism, which was the common trait of the painters of the period. This contraption caught the fancy of the public because of its technological character—a thing had to be scientific as well as mysterious in order to satisfy the contradictory taste of the Baroque, which, after all, developed not only the peep show but also the telescope and the microscope.

The public of the Baroque, then, must have gained a subtle and complex pleasure from looking at a *trompe l'œil*. For even familiar objects took on a new and haunting character through the heightened realism of their representation. The artist presented the commonplace with an esoteric taste in a technique that endowed it with a puzzling significance. It was therefore not accidental that one of the most ambitious *trompe l'œils* of the Baroque, Georg Haintz's *Kunstschrank* of about 1680, depicted a collector's cupboard.

The new development of the *trompe l'œil* had begun when the Dutch painter of animals, Melchior de Hondecoeter (1636-95), painted his *Dead Cock* (fig. 2). Like the partridge of de' Barbari, Hondecoeter's cock is suspended on a wall parallel to the picture plane, thus greatly enhancing the impression of being 'real.' The material of the wall is wood, and the grain is executed with minute care—a favorite device of the *trompe l'œil* from this time on. The Franco-Flemish painter Wallerant Vaillant employed this device in his *Letter Rack* of 1658 (fig. 3) showing a carefully portrayed grain of a wooden wall. Fastened to it by means of tape are a group of letters, a quill, and the knife for sharpening the quill. This new type of picture seems to have attracted attention at once, for only six years later it was imitated by the Dutchman Edward Colver. The letters, displayed with a tangible reality—one can read the addresses and an occasional line—arouse curiosity as to what they contain, merely because the painter has given them a commanding importance through his illusionistic representation. The spectator is puzzled; he senses a tantalizing secret, for the letters, despite their apparent reality, refuse to reveal their content.

The Flemish painter Norbert Gysbrecht enlarged the inventory of the *trompe l'œil* by introducing motifs from the cupboard and the library, and by combining them with the motif of 'Vanitas.' Among heavy volumes and all kinds of significant objects, including rosaries and watches, rests the ubiquitous skull, implying the futility of all the works of man. At the beginning of the eighteenth century, the Frenchman Jean-Baptiste Oudry embroidered on the types of the *trompe l'œil* as developed by Hondecoeter and Gysbrecht, and used them in the decoration of rooms, thus reviving a type of mural known to ancient Rome (fig. 6).

An anonymous English *trompe l'œil* dated 1717 was found at Oxford. It shows an odd assortment of prints and drawings spread on a board, evidently a development of the letter-rack type. Leopold Boilly in France painted a *trompe l'œil* of similar type at the end of the eighteenth century. The history of the *trompe l'œil* in Europe was brought to a conclusion shortly before the turn of the century by a few fruit pieces in *trompe l'œil* technique painted by the Swiss master Etienne Liotard, and after 1800 the technique disappeared from the creative stratum of European art. Neither Classicism nor Romanticism provided the psychological soil in which illusionism could flourish, for the first idealized the visible world and the second emphasized the forces of imagination. Naturalism and Impressionism, which followed these two movements, also were opposed to the idea of *trompe l'œil* because they suppressed detail in favor of pictorial unification. Consequently in Europe the *trompe l'œil* survived only sporadically, in the quaint efforts of some provincial painters, mostly amateurs.

The development of the objectivist still life took a road different from that of the *trompe l'œil*. At the beginning of the seventeenth century the Fleming Ambrosius Bosschaert picked up the thread of Gothic tradition that runs through the works of the Bruegel family. Very probably he was influenced by the great Pieter's son Jan, the so-called Velvet Bruegel, who was slightly older than he. Jan Bruegel's flower pieces, arranged mostly in the form of garlands, are executed in a miniaturelike style recalling the flowers in the margins of Flemish prayer books from the beginning of the sixteenth century. Bosschaert painted bunches of flowers in vases with the precision of Jan Bruegel, but he arranged his pictures in a strictly symmetrical manner that recalls Memling's objectivist flower piece. In the work of Jacob van Hulsdonck and other fruit painters, the same principles are to be found, though a careful balance replaces the strictly symmetrical arrangement of Bosschaert. Usually a bowl of glazed pottery stands on a table and is covered with apples, prunes, and grapes. Some fruits are placed in front of the bowl in a way that seems casual but that is in fact carefully designed, thus producing the impression of order and solemnity.

Dutch objectivism, it is true, was only an undercurrent in the history of still-life painting. Nevertheless it exerted an influence on the style of most of the masters of still life, including the whimsical Roeland Savery at the end of the sixteenth century and the lovable, though pedantic, Abraham Mignon in the second half of the seventeenth century.

With the popularization of science in the wake of the Enlightenment, a hundred years after Mignon's time, a new field was opened to objectivism: scientific illustration. Since mechanical methods of reproduction had not yet been invented, the artist was called upon to draw and paint illustrations for the new scientific books. At this period the link between science and art was still strong enough to make it imperative that a scientific illustration be not less artistic than accurate.

At this time, of all fields of science, botany most fascinated the amateur scientist of the day, who was the more influential because he belonged to wealthy society. Linnaeus' scientific achievement was still comparatively new, and it appeared a most urgent task to publish botanical encyclopedias to serve as guides to classification and comparative studies. They were printed in folios and illustrated with engravings, most of which were colored by hand. In their quest for illustrators, the publishers favored the most objective among the latest generation of Dutch flower painters.

The change from Rococo to the style of Louis XVI, which took place in the second half of the century, had a sobering effect on painting in general. Line began to supersede tone, and the flower painters who had kept up the tradition of Huysum gradually transformed it, under the influence of the classical taste of the time, into a smooth and precise decoration. It is significant that one of the outstanding Dutch flower painters of the time, Gerardus van Spaendonck (1746-1822), became a draftsman or 'professor of iconography' at the Jardin des Plantes in Paris. His occupation with the illustration of botanical works could not fail to influence his style as a painter, and such was the case with many other artists similarly engaged. It can even be taken for granted that botanical works as such affected the taste of both public and artist. In brief, the fruit and flower pieces that dominated still-life production around 1800 had a twofold development. They aimed at botanical correctness as well as the decorative effect necessary to match the neo-classical interiors of the period. This school, which I shall call 'botanic-decorative' spread all over Europe. Spaendonck's brother Cornelius (1756-1840), a designer for the porcelain factory at Sèvres, was instrumental in popularizing the style (fig. 11), for the products of Sèvres were considered models in the world of taste. But of course the new manner was also practiced by artists outside France. In England George Lance (1802-64), in Vienna Sebastian Wegmeyer, Franz Xaver Petter (1791-1866), Andreas Lach, and Anton Hartinger (1806-90) kept the botanic-decorative style alive in painting from the end of the eighteenth until late in the nineteenth century (fig. 12). The still lifes of this group are easily recognizable by their glassy texture, their hard colors, and their sharp outlines, as well as by their stiff composition—qualities that ought to be judged by the standards of the sober-minded society of their time.

Objectivism in Spain was raised to the level of the leading artistic stratum in Zurbarán's still lifes. He painted only a few, but his style lived on in a group of *bodegone* painters. Zurbarán imbued the objective still life with a dignity derived from his religious attitude toward life. There is no greater contrast of style possible than that between a Dutch breakfast piece, which creates sensuous delight, and the Zurbaran still life hanging in the City Art Museum of St. Louis (fig. 8). On a table parallel to the picture plane in the exact center of the painting is a basket of oranges and orange blossoms. It is flanked by a pewter plate with lemons and a cup and saucer, on which is another blossom. Every object is carefully outlined and strongly modeled. Each is a world of its own. This is no meal—it is, rather, an offering.

Among the still lifes by Zurbaran's followers the religious flavor is less marked. However, the symmetry and clarity of their compositions, as well as the linear and sculptural qualities, survive. Sometimes the Spanish *bodegone* recalls old-fashioned window displays.

The *bodegone* reached Mexico during the colonial period. Antonio Perez de Aguilar painted one there in 1786—testifying to the fact that objectivism in still-life painting survived in Mexico after it had disappeared in the mother country. This painting depicts with great simplicity and intensity the shelves of a pantry in a frontal view.

During the nineteenth century this style was rejected by the academic painters of Mexico and it found a refuge in the folk art. There are anonymous still lifes from the beginning to the middle of the century, which in all their naïveté have preserved a good deal of the dignity and order of ancient Spanish objectivism under a thin veil of contemporary taste (fig. 7).

Finally a few words about the fate of the 'close-up' type of still life. Dürer's 'foreground details' were imitated after his death, and these paintings remained popular collector's items all during the Baroque. Whether or not inspired by Dürer, the Dutchman Otto Marsaeus van Schrieck specialized in close-ups of underbrush, animated with reptiles and insects (fig. 5). This type of picture, which assumed an uncanny character in the hands of Marsaeus, was kept alive by his pupil, Mattheus Withoos, whose daughter and follower carried on the tradition into the eighteenth century. The English *genre* painter Alfred William Hunt did water-color close-ups of clumps of grass and birds' nests in the middle of the nineteenth century, but his minute, flawless technique is not without the sentimental approach reflecting the popular taste of the time.

The bulk of still-life production in Europe after the Baroque was of the picturesque type. This is true of the highly decorative hunting still lifes of the Rubens school, which like the Dutch flower paintings continued in a weakened form far into the eighteenth century.

In France, Chardin made a new start in the middle of the eighteenth century, reinterpreting the Dutch breakfast piece in terms of a new color scale. He mastered the richer palette of the Rococo style (fig. 10), adding his own observations to it, which led him close to the later discoveries of the Impressionists. A century later, Gustave Courbet resumed the naturalistic trend of Chardin, in his less-known fruit and flower pieces. In contradistinction to Chardin, Courbet retained the brown tonality of the Dutch masters. His still-life style inspired Carl Schuch (1846-1903), a Viennese member of the group gathered around Wilhelm Leibl in Munich (fig. 13). Not until Edouard Manet developed the technique of impressionism was Courbet's warm color scale replaced by that of bright daylight. Manet's still lifes of fruit and flowers with their patches of vivid color are the beginnings of a development that culminated in Renoir's flower pieces, the pure colors of which recall the hues of the rainbow.

Cézanne heralded a new era of the still life where color and form became the predominant values rather than light and texture. At the same time Van Gogh forced the still life to respond to his violent emotions. From the style of Cézanne and Van Gogh the post-impressionists developed their highly differentiated tendencies, which covered the range from pure abstraction to a mere distortion of reality. As early as the First World War, countercurrents to these movements began to evolve. The artists who led these movements called their groups *Valori Plastici* in Italy, *Neue Sachlichkeit* in Germany, and *Surréalisme* in France. Corresponding to their national backgrounds, the movement in Italy assumed a classical, in Germany a romantic, and in France a symbolic character.

All had in common a new emphasis on objects. The artist contemplated an isolated object until he perceived its very essence, and then, if possible, without copying from life, he projected it on the canvas as a self-contained creation. During the process of mental penetration, however, the object lost the familiar character of its part in daily life. It became charged with deeper meaning, with associations and implications, with symbolism and individuality. These overtones gave the work of art the quality that Franz Roh happily termed 'magic.' At one time the painter of the *trompe l'œil* had gained an uncanny effect from his peculiar illusionist technique. By similar devices in our time the 'Magic Realist' conjures up the impression that his dead objects are endowed with an enigmatic life of their own.

[9]

II. IN QUEST OF THE OBJECT

THE PHILOSOPHY that determined the intellectual attitude of the founders of the American republic was that of the French Enlightenment. Rationalism, marked by a lively interest in science, prevailed in the early years of the nation. A strikingly clear expression of this is found in the intellectual and artistic activities of Thomas Jefferson, whose interest in Greek and Roman architecture went hand in hand with his interest in technology, for the art of classical antiquity was considered at this time *the* rational art.

In painting, Charles Willson Peale represented a similar attitude. Born in Chestertown, Maryland, in 1741, he established himself in Philadelphia in 1776, where he died in 1827. Besides his artistic accomplishment he was also a natural historian and an illustrator of zoological books. Gerardus van Spaendonck, his French contemporary, developed what I have called the botanic-decorative style in painting while he was employed as a draftsman at the Jardin des Plantes in Paris. It is reasonable to assume that Peale's art was influenced by his work as a scientific illustrator, as was that of Spaendonck. However, Spaendonck was a still-life painter by profession, and Peale a portrait painter. Consequently, Peale did not develop the decorative qualities that distinguish Spaendonck and his school. Interest in natural history led him to methods of scientific representation outside the realm of painting. He established a museum, a sort of connecting link between the old curio cabinet, the art museum, and the natural history museum. In addition to a portrait gallery, Peale's museum housed collections of objects both pertaining to natural history and of general interest. It is less known, however, that Peale created the first 'habitat groups' for his museum, and thus anticipated a display technique of today's natural history museums. A 'habitat group' is a group of stuffed animals set up in an artificial landscape that imitates their natural home. For his stuffed specimens Peale painted landscape backgrounds that produced the illusion of reality.

It is significant that Charles Willson Peale practiced illusionism in his masterpiece, the so-called *Staircase Group* in the Philadelphia museum; this painting of his two eldest sons ascending a circular stairway achieves a deceptive degree of reality. It was originally framed in the woodwork of a doorway, with a carpeted step projecting below. Legend has it that he displayed it in the dimly lighted stairway of his house at the time of a visit from George Washington. The practical joke came off well, and, as the legend goes, the general waved a greeting to the two young Peales in the painting as he entered. Whether this story is true or not, Peale's zest for accuracy led him close to the *trompe l'œil*.

The American Revolution did not separate America from Europe culturally. American art still shared the unbroken Western tradition. Close intellectual ties connected the young republic especially with France, and as might be expected, this relationship was responsible for the development of similar patterns of art in the two countries. Accordingly, the botanic-decorative school of still life appeared in the New World as well as the Old. But in America, as in Europe, the development of still-life painting was contingent in its direction upon sufficient interest in independent artistic efforts. Without such interests there would have been inadequate incentive for the production of an art form such as still life, which appeals neither to human relations, as does the portrait, nor to other nonartistic qualities found in the subject matter.

In America this interest, and in turn the patronage necessary to it, did not evolve until the beginning of the nineteenth century, except in the case of John Singleton Copley (1737-1815) who introduced accessories in his portraits in a way that played up still-life motifs. A striking example is the bowl filled with apples from which the stout Mrs. Ezekiel Goldthwait, in her portrait at the Museum of Fine Arts in Boston, judiciously selects a luscious specimen. In fact the catalogue of an art exhibition held in Philadelphia as early as 1795 lists a number of still lifes by Copley and by other painters now forgotten. But none has been preserved, and even so, a few sporadic flower or kitchen pieces would only mean that European still lifes were known and occasionally imitated. Dutch settlers brought their paintings to America at an early date, presumably in the middle of the seventeenth century. Most of them, however, were discarded, for they were thought to be old-fashioned. Not until the end of the eighteenth century did a few eastern collections take shape, recovering the old works from the dust. It has been suggested that the origin of American still-life painting is found in these Dutch paintings, but a casual acquaintance with the art of the past is not enough to produce a new creative evolution. Furthermore, American painters in the early days were scarcely given to imitating the Old Masters. They strove rather to be up-to-date.

It was not a matter of chance that the history of American still-life painting began in the family circle of Charles Willson Peale, for here the conditions were most favorable. Peale often remarked that he was partly of French ancestry. He liked to speak French, and, like Benjamin Franklin, considered France his second country, at least intellectually. During visits to London he assimilated enough of the creative tradition of Europe to impart to his pupils a solid foundation; on the other hand, he had developed sufficient independence to overcome in his own teachings the limitations of his teacher, Benjamin West. West had become an orthodox European Classicist; he would not have shown much interest in the habitat groups of the strange museum organized by his pupil at Philadelphia. But the new ideas represented in the museum at Philadelphia were instrumental in stimulating what was eventually to develop into a real American style of painting. New ideas were assimilated and developed in the intellectual atmosphere created by Charles Willson Peale. Since the interests of father Peale included natural science, and since the current taste in America, no less than in Europe, was dominated by classicism, a basis was created for the growth of an objectivist art, especially since Peale's painting was distinguished by exact observation.

Born before the middle of the century, Charles Willson Peale arrived on the scene too early for the painting of more than a few still lifes as independent pictures, and these evidently were no more than studies of fruit. He was, however, practically the first American artist to include fully developed still-life motifs in his figure paintings. A good example is found in the group portrait of his family, begun in 1773 and completed in 1809, in which a carefully painted bowl of fruit is placed conspicuously on the table (fig. 14). It is a sound and forceful piece of painting; the volumes and the textures of the fruits are rendered convincingly.

Charles Willson Peale's younger brother James was, significantly, his pupil. James Peale was born in 1749. Still resilient enough in his sixties to grasp new ideas, he kept on painting up to his death in 1831. Although no dated still life by him antedates the eighteen-twenties, family letters of the Peales suggest that he began to paint others much earlier, perhaps about 1810. The development of his style cannot be analyzed with certainty until a dated still life of his early period is discovered. Yet it is reasonable to assume that those of his works painted in a broader and freer manner are of a later period than those done in a more detailed and timid style. If my conclusion in regard to the chronology of James's paintings is correct, his *Fruits of Autumn* (fig. 15) is one of his earlier works, for its style is wooden and strained as compared with the fluid and easy treatment of the dated works of his latest period.

James Peale's still lifes can be divided into two types: one shows vegetables or fruits piled on a table, illustrated here by a picture dated 1827, from the Pennsylvania Academy of Fine Arts (fig. 17); the other type, represented here by the *Fruits of Autumn*, has a bowl or a basket of fruit as its main motif. The receptacle is filled to overflowing with grapes, apples, and pears, and some of the fruits are placed on the table top. The edge of the table is parallel to the picture plane. An example dated 1825 is in the Worcester Art Museum (fig. 16). A bare wall forms the background of all these pictures. A subtle shading from light to dark, as John I. H. Baur points out, recalls the naturalistic lighting in Dutch interiors; but as employed by Van Huls-donck and other Dutch still-life masters of the seventeenth century, and especially as employed by James Peale, it is a purely arbitrary convention. Memling's flower piece established the pattern for this distribution of light and shadow as early as in the fifteenth century. Peale's demarcation between light and shade is invariably diagonal and more often than not it clashes with the direction of the light in the foreground. It serves to set off the bright and the dark sides of the still life to the best advantage, even though nature rarely produces such an effect.

This conventionalized chiaroscuro treatment of the background survived in the Dutch School in the works of the Van Spaendoncks (fig. 11); and it is found in the still lifes of the Viennese painter Franz Xaver Petter and other works of the botanic-decorative school (fig. 12). Thus it is not necessary to assume that James Peale had to go back to the old Dutch originals to learn the device. The use of botanic-decorative still lifes in the decoration of porcelain vessels may have been instrumental in making this style familiar to American artists, especially since English factories produced such ware.

Of the sons of Charles Willson Peale, Raphaelle, Rembrandt, and Rubens were predestined by their first names to become artists. Raphaelle, the eldest, must have been very close to his uncle James. Born in 1774, he was twenty-five years younger than James. We have to imagine that their relationship was first that of pupil and teacher, and that it only gradually changed into that of colleagues, who worked together and influenced each other. This conclusion is based on a comparison of their works. According to available records, which are meager enough, Raphaelle was trained by his father, but there can be no doubt that his uncle also contributed to his artistic education. The talents of both James and Raphaelle, it should be noted, led them in the same direction—the more so since their talents lay in miniature and still-life painting.

Raphaelle seems to have suffered much during his comparatively short life and he died in 1825, in his fifty-first year. Neither his portrait miniatures nor his still lifes gained him a livelihood. He was married and had children, but his father's letters reveal that poverty spoiled his family life. Gout affected his hands, and he spent his declining years in a tragic struggle against his growing incapacity, a fate recalling that of Renoir. The gout, it is said, caused him to abandon miniature painting in favor of still life, but some other cause must have been responsible for his change, for some of his mature still lifes display the same minute technique evidenced in the still lifes of his uncle James, the miniature painter. In fact, an untrained eye can scarcely distinguish between them. John I. H. Baur has compared the *Fruits of Autumn* (fig. 15) by James Peale, which belongs to the Whitney Museum of American Art, with Raphaelle's similar *Still Life with Peaches*, in the Brooklyn Museum (fig. 21). The two works invite comparison, since the china bowls containing the fruits seem to belong to the same set, and the same pattern of composition is to be found in both pictures. A detailed study reveals individual differences only if seen in magnified photographs, and these differences indicate that Raphaelle had a finer hand than James. To quote Baur:

His grapes are more solidly modelled, the highlights are worked in, and there is a gradual transition from light to shadow. The grapes of James's picture are more drily and at the same time more boldly handled. The contours are sharper, there is less range of tone and the highlights are crisply brushed, standing out as distinctly separate touches of white.

Dr. Baur concluded from this that Raphaelle used the same studio properties as his uncle, and everything speaks for the assumption that he took up still lifes under the influence of James—an influence that agreed with his own disposition. Raphaelle's illness certainly did not determine his choice of subject matter; but whether it impelled him to change his style is another question. Even if it did, the effect was not necessarily altogether destructive. It is well known, for example, that the development of Van Gogh, Aubrey Beardsley, and other artists reached its peak during a period of physical decay. Illness heightened the sensitivity of these artists. If the artist's disability does not prevent him from producing art, but only limits the range of his means of expression, this limitation may become a constructive element in so far as it forces the artist to be more direct, more concise, and more economical in his style.

Although we know that Raphaelle was given to drinking, only on the basis of exact information, which has not yet been forthcoming, can it be determined whether this habit contributed directly to his early death.

Raphaelle Peale's work is unassuming and small. Scarcely more than a few dozen little pictures are scattered through museums and private collections. Further investigation might find more, but it is doubtful that such a search would produce more impressive works. These modest paintings contain more strength than most of the more famous works of his contemporaries. What is it, then, that has led Raphaelle Peale's work into the limelight of the history of American art?

His first attempts at still-life painting were distinguished by an unusual intensity of observation and a deliberate concentration on the essential. The Historical Society of Pennsylvania has a still life of herring, and the Pennsylvania Academy of Art has two still lifes with fruit dated 1815. One of the latter shows apples, the other peaches, combined with grapes in a simple dish on a bare table seen in a strict frontal view: a strikingly objectivist arrangement (fig. 19). We shall be close to the truth if we date the beginnings of Raphaelle's work as a still-life painter in the period immediately preceding the year of these paintings. There is a still life, signed and dated October 1818, which shows a simple dish with a lemon, a grape, and wine leaves on a plain table. The background is a bare wall. The light comes from the left, but the left part of the background is dark—the conventional treatment of the chiaroscuro he had in common with his uncle James. However, the lemon and the grapes lack the solidity that distinguishes the fruits in James's paintings. The younger painter evidently was experimenting, for in the same year, 1818, he painted a still life far more advanced in technique: a medley containing raisins, berries, a sliced lemon, and biscuits grouped around a wine glass on an earthenware plate (fig. 20). The whole is placed on the inevitable bare table in front of a bare wall with the familiar arrangement of chiaroscuro. The work is much freer and broader; it has an arresting strength in the contrasts between light and darkness, but its style is still far from being fluid and sure. It is not even indicative of a hand used to miniature painting. Evidently Raphaelle was still feeling his way in this new branch of art.

The next few years seem to have been devoted to a development, the goal of which was to equal James. His illness must already have been acute, for it interrupted his work. We learn this from a letter of his father's dated 22 July 1821, in which he acknowledges the news of his son's temporary recovery. The still life with peaches that Mr. Baur used for a comparison with James's works was painted in the fall of the same year (fig. 21).

This painting shows the artist in full command of his medium. It is the perfect achievement of an objectivist *pur sang*. The decoration of the porcelain bowl, the skin of the peaches, the design of the leaves—everything is rendered with the utmost clarity and with a delight in recording the spherical shape of the peaches and the strict oval formed by the foreshortened rim of the porcelain bowl. It goes without saying that the table is seen directly from the front. The element of the picturesque is reduced to a minimum.

I assume that 1820 is the approximate date of the masterly still lifes of Raphaelle that show similar motifs, or of the variations in which a basket takes the place of the porcelain bowl. The year 1822, a letter from his father tells us, was a year of concentrated still-life production and even of slight financial success. The letters of the next year, however, reveal the father's increasing anxiety about the failing health and the desperate economic situation of his son. No further information has been forthcoming about the final years of the artist's life, but we can presume that his physical condition and financial misery gradually reduced his artistic production to a minimum.

In the first of his last three years, however, Raphaelle created his most important works. On 1 January 1822,

four months after the still life with peaches, Raphaelle signed a *Still Life with Cake*, now in the Brooklyn Museum, which deviates from the James Peale type, and seems almost to pick up the thread of Raphaelle's experimental years. A plate, scarcely visible, bears an apple, while raisins and leaves are spread over the rim. A piece of cake leans against the plate. The bright apple and the equally bright sugar coating of the cake form a strong contrast with the very dark background, which is dimly lighted with the barest suggestion of chiaroscuro at the right-hand corner. A cluster of dark raisins seems to creep into the foreground. The general impression is gloomy. The same year, 1822, produced the magnificent *Still Life with Watermelon* now in the Springfield Museum of Fine Arts, in which the painter gradually overcame his remaining picturesque traits (fig. 22). The bare, spherical body of the watermelon dominates the scene. It rests on a plate, which is seen in a sharply foreshortened view, with a grotesquely shaped slice of the melon lying alongside. The slice resembles the texture of a rock. The impression is that of bareness, of desolation, and by employing geometrical forms, the painter imparts a monumental character to a commonplace motif. Raphaelle's objectivism becomes almost a spiritual language. A strangely exaggerated precision in his late works approximates the illusionism of the *trompe l'œil*, and the choice and the arrangement of objects become more and more curious.

In the same year Raphaelle painted the *Still Life with Wild Strawberries* (fig. 23). A glass container is filled with neatly piled little berries. The foot of the glass container is hidden by a porcelain bowl containing hazel nuts and almonds, and a small bright apple, smooth as a billiard ball, tops it triumphantly. A dark branch of raisins slides sadly down to the bare table. A little farther back towards the dark background are a grotesque creamer and a squatty sugar bowl elevated by a pedestal of three superimposed saucers. All these heterogeneous household objects and fruits are sharply outlined and separately focused. They form an eloquent company whose silent conversation cries for a Hans Christian Andersen to put into words what might be a pathetic story of pride and prejudice.

I am inclined to date the charming *Still Life, Liqueur and Fruit*, which bears an illegible date, in the same year (fig. 24). It is closely related to the *Still Life with Wild Strawberries*, both in its composition and in details such as the treatment of glass and the bowl of fruit.

The *Still Life with Vegetables*, an unsigned and undated work now in the Wadsworth Atheneum, shows a drinking glass, half filled with water, containing the bare forms of onions and carrots (fig. 25). A more simplified still life, *Melons*, was painted perhaps a year later (fig. 26). They stick out from the water; their lower parts appear distorted by the refraction of the light. A grape without leaves is balanced on the rim of the glass. An apple and an oddly shaped tomato are on the table. The table, at variance with the usual style, is foreshortened. The chiaroscuro of the background is transformed into a severe division between light and shadow, and the configuration of this pattern in relation to the table produces an angular effect that is decidedly cubistic. Raphaelle's style has changed completely. There is no subtle rendering of textures. The picture looks almost primitive. Is it the result of Raphaelle's disability? Yes, in the sense in which a limitation is accepted as a challenge. For in this painting Raphaelle has fully developed a personal style that transcends the objectivism from which he set out, and that manifests a new power of abstraction. The utter simplification of the style suggests a very late date, probably the last two years of his life.

There is a unique painting by Raphaelle Peale that approaches still life in form: the painting *After the Bath*, signed and dated 1823 (fig. 28). A towel is spread over almost the whole picture area, and in a careful examination we find the arm and feet of a nude girl in the background. It is a striking and unconventional composition in which a decidedly banal subject is turned into a haunting, mysterious image. Symbolism? One feels a hidden meaning, a meaning that scarcely was intended or consciously expressed. A mere hint, a vague allusion lies in the fact that the view is obstructed by an object as ordinary as a bath towel. Its commonplace details, its folds and wrinkles, demand all our attention. Behind it extends a vast darkness. The towel maliciously forces itself between the painter and his model.

Raphaelle came as close to the *trompe l'œil* in this, his masterpiece, as his father once did in the *Staircase Group*, though from a different premise. The towel is seen in a strictly frontal view—an arrangement, as we have noted, favored by the *trompe l'œil* painters. This fact is significant, for it suggests that Raphaelle clung to the towel because it, and not the girl, was tangible reality to him, who lived on borrowed time. Thus he vested the towel with all the charm of his exquisite craftsmanship: it is a masterly still life in itself.

Shortly before his death in 1825, Raphaelle's work began to influence the family circle, though during his later years he himself seems to have been the object of pity rather than of admiration. His uncle James outlived him by six years, and the still lifes of his very old age definitely show the impact of Raphaelle's work.

Baur justly points out that the *Still Life, Fruit* by James Peale in the Worcester Art Museum, dated 1825, shows the growing influence of the nephew on the uncle (fig. 16). It shows 'a rich chiaroscuro, a subdued color and relatively simple composition in contrast to his more characteristic high key and rather elaborately baroque arrangement.'

An important still life of James's, *Watermelon and Grapes* (fig. 18), now at the Wadsworth Atheneum, shows a partly sliced watermelon on a large earthenware bowl; a dark and a light grape complement the large bulk of the melon. James Peale here emphasized the geometric elements of the melon in the manner of Raphaelle: the ovals of the foreshortened slices are outlined with deliberate exactitude. The knife that did the slicing still sticks in the pulp of the gigantic fruit, pitiless, sharp, mechanical. With their cleanly outlined circles, the little balls of the grapes form an appropriate accompaniment. The huge dark body of the melon is contrasted dramatically with the dim light on the brighter side of the plain background.

Although stronger and more severe in atmospheric treatment of light and texture than *Still Life, Fruit* (fig. 17), which bears the date 1827, *Watermelon and Grapes* is sufficiently related to it to lend support to the fairly old but not necessarily authentic inscription '1824' found on the latter.

In the Boston Museum of Fine Arts a remarkable picture attributed to James Peale on the basis of verbal tradition shows a large bowl of fruit on a table covered with a white cloth (fig. 30). It introduces a principle unheard of at the time of James Peale: the objects are seen from above so that the horizon is high up in the picture. By means of this device, which Europe learned from the Japanese, and that not until the period of the impressionists, the foreshortening of perspective is reduced, so that the elements of the picture are distributed in the form of a surface pattern.

Not only the revolutionary arrangement of the picture but also its soft tonality strikes us as something unfamiliar in James Peale's work—not to speak of the tablecloth and a blue napkin motif that appears nowhere else in James's paintings. Hence we cannot ignore the possibility that this might be the work of a hitherto unknown artist who further developed James Peale's style, possibly a pupil.

Another unsigned still life that recently came to light, shows some points of similarity with the *Bowl of Fruit*. A wicker basket with grapes and peaches forms its main motif (fig. 31). To the right is a glass half filled with water. A silver spoon is in front of the basket, and a few coins—apparently French—are in front of the glass. The objects are on a plain, brown table, and stand out from a black background in a sharp light—almost Caravaggio-like. Both form and texture have been executed with a keen eye. The firmness of the modeling, the boldness of the composition, and the chiaroscuro are general characteristics that the *Wicker Basket* has in common with the *Bowl of Fruit*. There is one detail in particular distinguishing them from the rest of the still lifes that were identified with James and Raphaelle Peale: the illustration of table silver and its pictorial treatment. The silver spoon in the *Wicker Basket* corresponds to the silver knife in the *Bowl of Fruit*. In both cases the reflection of the metal is studied as a pictorial problem in a way considerably ahead of the stage of evolution reached by the Peales in their known works. A closer observation reveals that the painters of the two pictures—if they were not the same person—emphasized the effect of reflected light throughout their composition, as illustrated by the lightened shadow on the right side of the porcelain bowl in the one, and by the touch of light on the right side of the basket over the spoon in the other.

Raphaelle's younger brother Rubens, born in 1784, did not enjoy anything like the attention received by Raphaelle. Although he lived to the age of eighty-one, little is known about his life, except that he followed his father in organizing museums. He seems to have taken up painting late, after he resigned from the museum in New York, about 1837, and moved to Pottstown, Pennsylvania. His daughter Mary Jane, who was a competent painter, might have stimulated him to try his hand at painting. Rubens was not an artist of great technical skill—perhaps it was for this reason that he was not taken very seriously by his contemporaries. Many of his paintings are close imitations of the works of James and Raphaelle; but they are greatly simplified, and indicate that he did not understand the details of perspective. There is, however, a quaint charm in his work, a disarming ingenuity suggesting a fine and sensitive personality. And indeed, when he freed himself from the models of his brother and his uncle and set out to paint an arrangement of his own, he achieved startling results. It is true, though, that the Douanier Rousseau had to create his naive masterpieces before his humble predecessor, Rubens Peale, could be appreciated. It is interesting to note that both he and the great Frenchman did not undertake painting until late in life.

The name of Henri Rousseau is called to mind by a work of Rubens Peale's which in subject matter is not a still life in the strict sense: *Two Grouse in Underbrush of Laurel* (fig. 33). It was painted, according to an inscription on the back of the canvas, in 1864. On the background of a highly conventionalized pattern of foliage the two birds are perched stiffly. Their plumage is definitely stylized, and their appearance is strangely lifeless, as if they were stuffed birds. It is not improbable that Rubens Peale was inspired by one of the habitat groups of his father; the result was a picture that approximates a still life rather than a landscape with living animals. It will be recalled that the Douanier Rousseau created similar close-ups of imaginative jungles with toylike birds.

There is a *Flower Piece* by Rubens Peale that bears the date 1856 (fig. 32), and that shows a marked similarity to the style of *Two Grouse in Underbrush of Laurel*. The *Flower Piece* shows a porcelain bowl with open work resembling the bowls used by James and Raphaelle Peale. A circular cartouche in the center of the bowl shows the inscription 'RP to CWP' and the year. The initials 'CWP' designate Rubens's son, Charles Willson Peale, for whom the picture was painted. On the back of the painting are the words 'Rubens Peale from Nature in the Garden, 1856,' written in what is believed to be the artist's own handwriting. The garden flowers in variegated array are treated in a decorative manner, though they were avowedly painted from nature. They form a pattern, almost symmetrically filling the space of the painting with scarlet cactus flowers, yellow and orange gaillardia with brown centers, and blue and crimson blossoms of various species. Pink, yellow, and red roses contrast with the white of a calla lily. The evidence of his *Flower Piece* indicates that Rubens Peale was genuinely naive in his attitude toward nature, but that he was not without some training.

A third painting deserves to be considered a part of the same group of Rubens's works, since it is relatively independent of the models of James and Raphaelle. It is a 'table piece' known under the name of *The American Dessert* (fig. 34). It is signed, but not dated. A decanter with glasses on a round tray; a sugar-coated cake on a white plate with a crocheted cover; a porcelain basket ('second Rococo') filled with raisins; another with hazel nuts; a group of walnuts, a giant nutcracker and some half-cracked nuts, some of which are set on a small plate with a nut-pick—all are assembled to form a complex composition in front of a bare background. The direction of the light is the same in the foreground as in the background—proof that Rubens, in all his naïveté, has overcome the last traditional formula, which Raphaelle had not abandoned. There is something very touching, very gentle, very engaging in the picture. It appears almost artless in comparison with Raphaelle's style.

James's daughter Sarah Miriam (1800-1885) carried on the family tradition, painting watermelons with the courageous bareness introduced by Raphaelle, but without the strange overtones that made Raphaelle's realism 'magic.' Her realism, rather, was a parlor realism. She composed a still life (fig. 29) in an oval frame as if it were a family portrait—and who knows? perhaps, in a symbolic sense, it was. She probably did not know that Chardin had done the same in his period, which had inherited the use of oval picture frames from the Baroque (fig. 10).

There were more painters in the family, Anna Claypole Peale (1791-1878) and Margaretta Angelica Peale (1795-1882), James's daughters, whose works are very similar to those of Sarah, but somewhat more uncertain (fig. 36). Rubens Peale too had a daughter who painted: Mary Jane Peale (1826-1902) (fig. 38). And finally there were James G. Peale (1823-91) and Washington V. Peale (1825-68), James's grandsons, who painted only as a hobby but nevertheless with good taste and a pleasant, if only small, talent. Their studies of birds and plants represent the family tradition in its last diluted stage.

Even the initial stage in the development of the 'Peale style,' roughly 1815 to 1820, prompted contemporary imitation. In Philadelphia, Robert Street, who was a half-primitive and half-professional portrait painter, produced a still life in 1818: *Fruit in Basket* (fig. 27). The composition is somewhat anemic but the honesty of the little work makes it attractive.

The great virtue of the American primitive artist is honesty, which he inherited from the American craftsman—if, indeed, he was not a craftsman himself. There was no sharp line between the strata of artists. Numerous painters developed from sign painting, as often happened, incidentally, in ancient Holland. In 1821 or even earlier one of the successful sign painters of Philadelphia, J. A. Woodside, was painting still lifes in the style of the Peales. They show fruits grouped in and around a basket. The style is heavy and betrays Woodside's decorative training, but the firmness, the solidity, and the consistent treatment of the form are convincing enough to make up for the stiffness. His son Abraham (1819-53) painted still lifes in the style of his father (fig. 35). The Woodsides form the connecting link between the *avant-garde* school of the Peales and the American primitives.

This link between the Peale tradition and primitive art turned out to be of an astonishing longevity, surviving as late as the early twentieth century. George Cope (1855-1929), a semi-primitive painter in Chester County, near Philadelphia, created still lifes that in their fastidious style outdo the sharply focused forms of Raphaelle Peale, of whose work they are vaguely reminiscent (fig. 37). His irregular perspective and the isolated effect of the elements of his composition distinguish him from the more academic artists of his period. A work like his *Still Life* of 1913, with a watermelon, a cantaloupe, apples, grapes, and a pear, is objectivist in an ingenuous way.

III. PRIMITIVES AND AMATEURS

IT HAS been noted that numerous early American artists of high professional standing began their careers as humble sign painters. This could not have been otherwise in a new country with a predominantly agricultural population. The craftsman supplied the needs of the community, and what was called the 'fine arts' was a luxury patronized only by wealthy planters in the South and merchants in eastern cities. Outside of Boston, New York, and Philadelphia, scarcely an opportunity was given for the study of art; and even in these three centers, the facilities were far from satisfactory. It was this almost medieval situation that produced the phenomenon of the American primitive. This term was well chosen to designate the works of untrained artists whose background was that of the craftsman, for the background of the medieval primitive was similar. The crafts belong to a stratum of civilization that up to the industrial revolution was essentially static. The very oldest techniques of the world lived on in the work of the carpenter, the blacksmith, the stonemason; and along with the techniques, a stock of basic decorative motifs was bequeathed from one generation to another. An American sign painter or woodcarver learned his trade in a way quite similar to that of the artisans in ancient Europe, and this way included the basic principles of design. The result is an art that scorns perspective and correct draftsmanship, but is distinguished by directness of expression and soundness of structure.

When a painter succeeded in raising his standard from the level of folk art to that of professional art, his success was a proof of his talent, but remaining a primitive was by no means proof of a lack of skill. It could be owing simply to a lack of opportunity, a reason that was very prevalent in remote areas. Many of the primitive paintings of America are attractive because they are simply the works of people who had talent but no training. A comparison with Europe, where the opportunities of an art education were almost general, is not conclusive. True, Europe produced greater artists, but on the other hand it had almost no primitives in the nineteenth century; the stratum of its population that formerly had produced the delightful folk and peasant art evidently had been converted into the mass of the 'artistic proletariat,' which since has clogged the art centers in the big cities of Europe.

It is known that some of the Dutch Old Masters began as sign painters, and from the fact that many of them excelled as still-life painters, the conclusion is often drawn that Dutch still-life painting grew from the humble profession of sign painting. The history of art, however, shows that still-life painting developed from *genre* painting in Holland. The interest in accessories gradually increased to such a degree that the accessories gained precedence over the actions of the figures in the painting, even though they might be Biblical characters. There was only one step from this stage to making the accessories the exclusive object of an artistic representation.

The situation was different in America. There were very few still-life motifs in the portraits of the colonial period, and there was very little historic or *genre* painting that could have been a preliminary stage of still-life painting. In the realm of the fine arts, I have shown that American still-life painting was part of an international movement, which was linked to the study of natural history: the botanic-decorative school. This could not have been the case in the realm of primitive art. Nevertheless, around 1800, at least some primitive still lifes were being painted, as illustrated by the *Bountiful Board*, now in the Rockefeller Collection, Williamsburg, Virginia. This is a strongly conventionalized table piece with drapery around it. The still life is painted on canvas; otherwise it might have been an actual inn sign. But only its decorative character and its subject matter suggest the latter. Painted inn signs are easily lost in the course of time, but occasionally one sees at an antique dealer's a still life with a bottle and some victuals that possibly once served as a sign of good cheer outside a tavern. Such pictures are more or less artless, and are not likely to be old. They suggest, however, that similar unpretentious representations may have preceded them; the men who produced them were the old sign painters. There is a lithograph, *Mortgaging the Farm*, which dates from the eighteen forties and shows an inn sign with a fruit on it. The print appeared at the firm of D. W. Kellog and Co. but does not show the signature of the artist. The sign which, according to its inscription, offers 'Entertainment for Man and Beast' in a near-by 'dram shop,' is decorated with a big grape. This representation is too late to prove that there were still lifes on inn signs in America before still-life painting became an independent art form. It makes it only probable.

Whether the inn sign contributed to the origin of still-life painting in America remains an open question, since no example of really old inn signs with still lifes are known, but at least one type of still life had a predecessor in an earlier stratum of art in America: the flower piece. It appeared in a limited area, Pennsylvania, and its style was the highly formalized so-called 'Fractur.' 'Fractur' is the popular name applied to the Pennsylvania German illustrated manuscripts or 'Fracturschriften.' Edith Gregor Halpert described the Fractur as follows: 'The word refers specifically to a Gothic letter, but as a medium, "Fractur" is a quill drawing tinted with home-made dyes applied with a cat's-hair brush. Both a survival and a revival of European medieval book illumination,' which in turn was saturated with much older Near Eastern elements, 'Fractur was taught as early as 1730 in Ephrata,' seat of a Pietist congregation. 'It flourished throughout the state among related sects until the middle of the nineteenth century, when the printed "Taufscheine" and other documents replaced the highly decorative originals. . . Similar designs incorporating the traditional tulip, birds . . . , apparently religious in significance, appear in various combinations, and were used not only in the illuminated manuscripts, but also for decorating dower chests, furniture, kitchen utensils, pottery, coverlets, and other household objects. . . Although commonly referred to as a Book-mark or "Lese-zeichen," the "Stylized Flowers" is probably a color design for use as a sample' (fig. 39).

The examples of Fractur as applied in decorating furniture and other things from daily life were spread widely. It would be fruitless, however, to try to relate directly to Pennsylvania Fractur any nineteenth-century American primitives who approximate the decorative qualities of Fractur, though they do not share its iconography.

Many traditions blended in the primitive stratum of American art, and the earlier the examples the more they suggest a comparison with the old popular forms of decorative art in Europe. Hellenistic mosaics, for example, are suggested by a pastel (fig. 43), a still life of multicolored fruit arranged before a black background in a totally unnaturalistic manner on and around a table with a much too big singing bird perched on a leaf. It has a distinctly Mediterranean flavor, and reflects the Italian taste. One is inclined to date this puzzling and unique work around 1800.

There is a still life with the signature 'Chipman,' a name otherwise unknown, which illustrates impressively both the quality and the limitations of a primitive still-life painting (fig. 41). A rough table is covered with fruits: two cantaloupes and two watermelons, one of which is sliced. A banana is placed on the cantaloupes, and a vine with grapes and leaves is spread over the fruits. The semicircles of the watermelon slices and the patterns of the seeds form the nucleus of a composition that is not without decorative strength. Evidently the painter was needy; for he painted a frame on the borders and the sides of his canvas—achieving a very naive sort of *trompe l'œil*. No direct link connects this work with the refined sphere of the Peales. It is American folk art, and as such it bears an affinity to primitive still-life painting in general, and to the Pennsylvania German art even less than to art provinces outside the United States. A comparison with the work of an unknown Mexican painter from Queretaro, which was published by Roberto Montenegro in his book on *Mexican Painting*, demonstrates this coincidence. It is dated 1851. As in the painting by Chipman, a sliced watermelon on the right side is the geometric unit around which the other fruits are grouped to form a decorative design; also the fruits are arranged in horizontal layers and cover almost all the picture space. Even the motif of the painted frame is common to both pictures.

There are all kinds of primitive still lifes: some attract attention through their childlike ingenuity but are too clumsy to be taken seriously, and some approach the style of the professional painter, as is the case with a charming fruit and flower piece signed by an otherwise unknown painter, Adèle Evans, the fluid and tonal style of which suggests the period from 1830 to 1840 (fig. 42). Only the faulty perspective and the exaggerated attention paid to the grain of the marble table and other ornamental details reveal its fundamentally primitive standard.

The love of ornament and pattern occasionally lures the primitive painter into fashioning flowers and fruits after the model of the decorative products of his time, and such foreign elements of pseudosophistication are always in distinct contrast to the general character of his product. In general, oil painting is not the best medium for a primitive painter; in fact, it was developed in the fifteenth century as a medium to overcome the limitations of a genuinely primitive period, i.e. the art of the Middle Ages. Thus the American primitive of the nineteenth century is much more at ease when he restricts himself to water colors, which easily lend themselves to a decorative treatment. He also attains very satisfactory results, without exceeding the limits of his talent, when he devotes himself to purely decorative tasks, as in the case of velvet painting. This technique is often, but not at all regularly, synonymous with the so-called theorem painting, which consists of applying predesigned motifs on velvet or other materials by means of stencils. The use of stencils allows the imagination of the artist only a limited range.

The first half of the nineteenth century was the era of the amateur. Mechanization had not yet offered humanity standardized means of recreation. If one wanted art or music at home, he had to contribute most of it himself. This involved the training of one's talents, great or small, and this training not only led to the production of innumerable engaging though unpretentious works of art, but also made people art conscious in general.

Sometimes a written statement preserved for us by a happy accident allows us to glance into the atmosphere in which this art grew. There is a delightful water color of a still life with flowers and fruits that for a short time appeared from its hiding place in some attic to disappear only too quickly into a private collection (fig. 44). This 'chef d'œuvre inconnu,' bore a touching inscription on the back of its old wooden board. The inscription runs: 'Wedding present from her affectionate husband Amory L. Babcock. Drawn and colored from Nature by Amory L. Babcock.' Nothing is known about the artist, but the few words he wrote in a meticulous and elegant handwriting give us a clue to the cultural standing of the amateur artist in his period. The work is dated 1857.

Babcock's water color shows a brown basket with reddish zinnias on a table covered with a green cloth. Oranges and lemons painted in vigorous local colors are on the table. Against the steel blue sky, which forms the greater part of the background—the rest is covered by a brown drapery—is a yellow butterfly. The color scheme is bold, practically unique in its time. The drawing shows a strong tendency to stylization and betrays the layman in the failure of its attempt to convey volume. As a whole, the picture looks like the product of an imaginative designer who works from memory and is not averse to incorporating standard types of decorative flowers in his composition. His disregard of atmosphere, shadows, reflections, and whatever else a naturalistic painter records when he represents reality add to this impression, which, however, is deceptive, for the painter expressly stated that he painted from nature. We must conclude from this testimony that a genuinely primitive artist unconsciously transformed nature into a strikingly formalized image. He could help it no more than an Egyptian or Byzantine painter could, when he conventionalized his figures according to what seems to us a rigid canon. Babcock's humble inscription is of general interest, for it confirms the fact that primitive art can be produced in the same way as 'advanced' art, i.e. by studying nature. The well-known sketch book of the Gothic architect Villard de Honnecourt shows that a medieval artist recorded what he saw in terms of an almost abstract design. This idea is foreign to most of us, who have inherited the attitude towards reality which came to prevail in the nineteenth century, but it was a matter of course with the amateur artist only a century ago.

Finally the short inscription teaches us another valuable lesson: a young bridegroom considered it an adequate expression of his devotion to paint a picture as a wedding present. The move presupposes a similar attitude on the part of the bride, for otherwise her 'affectionate husband' would have resorted to more material tokens of his love. Thus we see that the taste of the amateur artist, with its merits and limitations, must have been a pretty well established artistic attitude in America before the Civil War. It must be concluded from this observation that the work of primitive painters was a legitimate stratum in American art; and that since it produced significant works of a distinct character, this stratum contributed essential elements to American art as a creative movement.

On the basis of the examples I have discussed so far, the qualities that are common to the Peales and the amateur still-life painters appear to be the exactitude and geometrism of style, and an ingenuous directness in grasping the visual world.

Amory L. Babcock, it must be conceded, was a man of unusual talent. Most of the other amateur water colors that have been preserved are less striking, but they include such delightful specimens as the *Flowers on Black Marble Table* (fig. 45), of about 1835, which in its formalized arrangement recalls the flower compositions of the Spaendoncks and other botanic-decorative painters, but in detail betrays the naive background of the painter. No doubt the artist, like Amory L. Babcock, studied his flowers 'from nature.'

Thomas Sully (1787-1872), in a charming portrait of two young women, a Mrs. Boyd and a Mrs. Smith, has bequeathed to us a vivid document that corroborates Amory L. Babcock's statement about the method of painting employed by the amateur (fig. 47). The young lady in the foreground holds a portfolio with the inscription 'Sketches from Nature,' above the painter's signature 'T S' and the date 1823. On the table, to the right, is a bunch of flowers in a round glass vase; the bunch of flowers with its rose in the center and its tulip on top is typical of the 'Lady's Work' of the time, i.e. decorative water colors and velvet paintings (fig. 46). Evidently the bunch of flowers is one of the models of the *Sketches from Nature* which the young lady with the intelligent and lovely face—very classic indeed—is about to open.

A similar bunch of flowers is the model of the artistic endeavors of a boy portrayed in a miniature by the American painter Ann Hall (1793-1863), who illustrated this scene in a family portrait with herself as one of the group.

There are velvet paintings evidently based on water colors, and the latter were, as illustrated above, often painted with the model in front of the artist (figs. 50 and 48). The stylization of the flowers came quite naturally to the amateur painter; it was not strictly caused but nevertheless was influenced by his familiarity with the decorative art of his time. There are also velvet paintings like the primitive fruit pieces represented by Chipman's *Still Life with Melons and Grapes* (fig. 41). Many of the velvet paintings, it is true, are stylized versions of models taken consciously from examples of professional art and are only flavored by the genuine primitivism of their makers. Baur has demonstrated that some velvet painters copied works of James Peale in a more or less faithful way, and that the changes undergone by the model in the process of being copied are to be attributed mainly to the adaptations required by the coarser technique and the limitations of the medium. It has been shown, furthermore, that at least one type of velvet flower painting was derived from a contemporary flower painting via the medium of a popular lithograph. The type of the contemporary painting is again that of Spaendonck, and that means the botanic-decorative school. The precision and texture of the model, it is true, could not be retained in the medium of velvet. The decorative tendency of the school however was not only preserved but emphasized and developed in a new direction. The freedom granted to the velvet painter by the combination of stencils and by variations of the given themes, as well as by the selection of color, produced effects often strikingly similar in their two-dimensionality to those of old Chinese color prints. Chinese woodblocks at the time were still unknown to the West.

On the other hand, some European Baroque motifs reappeared in a simplified form, among them the overturned bowl, which was popular with the late Dutch still-life painters. Abraham Mignon carefully supplied motivation for the use of this motif by introducing a cat which, on its hunt for a mouse, overturns a flower vase. The American velvet painters—mostly girls who acquired the feminine brand of aesthetic culture in a finishing school—took such motifs for granted and used them naively. They drew the motifs from prints that were commonly known under the name of the drawing master who offered them for sale. Such a velvet painting is illustrated here (fig. 49). Its pattern was known as the 'Haviland Velvet,' from the designer's name.

Some of the velvet paintings are formalized to a degree that classifies them with objects of a purely decorative character. They form a connecting link with other branches of amateur art, such as the making of pictures with tin foil and embroidery.

Tinsel paintings and embroideries were in part derived from the same models as velvet paintings, but they were also inspired by conventional types of flower arrangements, especially bouquets, wreaths, and garlands. Since embroideries and tinsel paintings were given to friends as tokens of friendship or as keepsakes, it was only natural that they employed the types of flower arrangements connected with significant conventions, including the wreath, which decorates the door at Christmas and on other festive occasions, or the nosegay, which accompanies the birthday visit as well as the marriage proposal.

The humble products of tinsel painting and pictorial embroidery form the connecting link between painting in the higher sense of the word and such artless products as the pictures that accompanied dedications in the albums of the romantic lady or enhanced the eloquence of the valentine—the last refuges of the unsophisticated variety of flower piece.

IV. ROMANTIC INFLUENCES

DURING the first half of the nineteenth century the boundaries between primitive and professional painting in America were not defined. It was not seldom that an itinerant 'limner,' who to all practical purposes was a primitive, found comparatively late in life an opportunity to acquire formal training, and eventually opened a studio in one of the larger towns. It ought to be kept in mind that portrait painting before the advent of photography was a profitable profession in places where life had become settled and where wealth was growing. The New England portrait painter S. Harvey Young offers a good example of such a development, since we are acquainted with portraits of his primitive period as well as of his later years when he was a well-established portrait painter in Boston. His early works show the distortions and hardness typical of the untrained artist, but they also display an ingenuous charm and a quality of design that the professional and correctly drawn portraits of his Boston period do not possess.

With the growth of the American cities, art instruction was more easily obtainable and more widely spread. The stratum of primitive painting first receded from the urban centers and finally disappeared except for isolated instances of painters who lived in the backwoods or belonged to culturally underprivileged groups. Only a modicum of primitivism survived in a number of paintings, most of which were done by anonymous artists, and even this often shades into mere provincialism.

Still, not all talented Americans aspired to the rank of professionals in the middle of the nineteenth century. Many of them remained amateurs, although they had acquired much more technical skill in the rendering of nature than their primitive predecessors. Numerous manuals of painting were published in the United States at this time, and their success was attested by a large group of educated people who seriously studied art either by themselves or under the more or less competent guidance of the drawing master. There is a fundamental difference between the training of the sign painter as an apprentice and the academic training of the professional artist. Whereas the first method is based on the tradition of the craftsman and develops the gift of design, the latter sets up a close imitation of nature as the goal of the student and has a vaguely classic taste as its aesthetic principle. The educational ideal of the time was to be as closely in touch with Europe as possible. Although very proud of their political independence, the Americans of pre-Civil War days felt themselves part and parcel of Western civilization. It was just this attitude that prevented them from identifying themselves with the art of a single European nation. They went to European art centers to study, but with few exceptions did not attempt to become French, German, or Italian painters, as did the expatriates of the next generation. They were naive enough not to see the whole problem, for nationalism had not yet colored the thinking of men. They simply strove to paint well, and that they did with considerable success. It is true that the application of European training to the American scene sometimes proved difficult for the artist after his return from overseas; one of the best American painters of the period, Worthington Whittredge (1820-1910), gave a forceful expression of this conflict in his autobiography. He wrote:

Schools of art are the result of the slow accumulation of work done by many men . . . who, in the aggregate, stamp the work of their period with a national or local character. . . If America is ever to receive any distinctive character so that we can speak of an American School of Art, it must come from this new condition, the close intermingling of the peoples of the earth in our peculiar form of government.

Although it makes the creation of a distinctly American art its goal, Whittredge's statement is fundamentally at variance with nationalist aesthetics. His program came closer to realization in his own time than he knew, for the works of the best among his contemporaries, at least in our eyes, have acquired a distinctly American flavor; the milieu in which they lived not only conditioned the subject matter of their paintings but, in a subtle way, filled them with an unmistakably American atmosphere.

The new generation of artists grew up in the transitional period between romanticism and realism. Both movements were international, and the 'time lag' that later on characterized the relation between American and European art had not yet developed. Now, romanticism was not interested in still life, for its very goal was drama, passion, phantasy—qualities that demanded as subject matter, if not man himself, then at least a landscape in which to project feelings and conflicts. Not until a new vogue of realism had developed did still lifes gain a renewed interest for the painter. True, the Peale family kept on painting still lifes in their own way, romanticism or no romanticism; but from the historical point of view, these artists were a living anachronism. Their work descended from the position of *avant-garde* art into that of a conservative undercurrent. It catered to people who were equally anachronistic—such people exist in every period and are supported by the survivors of an older generation who are conservative by nature; hence the Peales had their patrons even in the third quarter of the nineteenth century, patrons who enjoyed their objectivist attitude, out of date though it was.

The new generation, however, did not approach the world with the naive rationalism of their grandfathers, who had been young at the apex of the Enlightenment. A Thomas Jefferson, designing the Capitol of Virginia, could still consider the Greek temple the best possible architectural expression of modern democracy. A John A. Roebling, designing the Brooklyn Bridge, abandoned the classic style. He used Gothic forms, which came closer to the new engineering architecture. A Benjamin West never abandoned the 'grand manner' so dear to the classic taste, even though his subject matter was taken from American history. A George Caleb Bingham, on the other hand, painted the Mississippi boatmen and the crowds of Kansas City on election day exactly as he saw them, without any pretense of grandeur.

The fact that Roebling selected Gothic forms for his bridge not only attests to the compatibility of Gothic forms with those of steel construction, but also suggests that romanticism tinged the artistic thinking of the generation of realism to which Roebling belonged. For the Gothic revival is an expression of romanticism in architecture.

The term 'romantic realists' has been coined for the painters who in the middle of the nineteenth century painted scenes of everyday life, both in Europe and in America. Their realism was modified by emotional overtones. This is the quality that strikes us as romantic. The stylistic evolution led from the linearity of classicism to the tonality of the romanticists.

The romantic realists went farther in the development of a tonal style than their truly romantic predecessors like Washington Allston; for the latter could not quite dissociate themselves from the manner of their classicist teachers. For still-life painting, that means a revival of the picturesque type so popular in the seventeenth and eighteenth centuries. The change, however, was not sudden.

There is a small painting of a salad dish by an unknown artist, which, judging from its style, might have been painted around 1830 (now in the Karolik Collection, Boston). Its technique and draftsmanship reveal considerable training, and the picture strikes us as revolutionary in its decidedly realistic approach. Almost the whole canvas is filled by a plain dish containing lettuce and sliced eggs and an ordinary fork. Crisp brushwork reveals the intense concentration of the painter. One has to go far in the nineteenth century before finding an equally monumental still life—Jean François Millet and Vincent van Gogh painted potatoes and fruits of a character suggesting their anonymous American predecessor. The nearest approach in the art of that time was made in Mexico, where an anonymous painter in about 1800 painted a wooden table covered with rustic dishes. This picture, reproduced by Roberto Montenegro in his book on Mexican painting, gives a solemn effect. It could be the table at which Christ and the Disciples sat down for the Last Supper. The spirit of Zurbarán lives in it. The American painting is much less solemn—but both pictures reflect a pious attitude towards food. Grace is said before the meal is touched.

It is not known where the *Salad Dish* was painted, and speculation is difficult, since its highly individual style shows no similarity to that of any of the familiar painters of the period.

Still lifes were painted either by portrait and *genre* painters in their spare time, or by artists who specialized in still lifes. There was some demand for still lifes as decoration. Of the New England portrait painter Jeremiah Pearson Hardy (1800-1888), for instance, a relative of his has recorded that 'he often painted fruit pieces, either to fill a demand for dining-room pictures or to preserve for some horticulturist the record of some especially good specimen he had produced.' Few of his paintings are known today: one that has survived in a faded photograph shows a few apples on a barrel; another shows three pears between grapes (fig. 61). This small picture is painted in a broad and direct technique, which reflects the influence of S. F. B. Morse, with whom Hardy studied after preliminary training under a local Boston artist, for Morse had achieved a considerable degree of pictorial freedom in his portraits.

After 1850, photography began to compete seriously with portrait painting. As a consequence, many portrait painters took up still-life painting on the side; more often than not still lifes signed by well-known portrait painters date from the second half of the nineteenth century.

The Long Island master of homespun *genre* scenes, William Sidney Mount (1807-68), left us a few flower studies; one of them is illustrated here (fig. 52). It shows a loosely bound bunch of black-eyed Susans, daisies, roses, and other spring flowers. It is distinguished by an engaging directness and vividness, and it convincingly conveys the feeling a sensitive observer experiences on a beautiful May day, as he looks at the humble flowers he has picked on a walk through the fields. In all its realism this modest sketch has the romantic fragrance of a *Lied* by Schubert.

It has been mentioned above that Philadelphia produced the most important school of still-life painters. The folk art of the Pennsylvania Germans created a favorable atmosphere for still-life painters. It stimulated the sense of design; it inspired interest in decoration. Boston, the second of the two oldest centers of cultural life, patronized the art of the English upper classes. This art was refined and individualistic and its dominant interest was the portrait. It is significant that the Peales settled in Philadelphia, not in Boston. The activity of the Peales encouraged other painters to take up still-life painting and since their time the tradition has not died.

Among the portrait painters of Philadelphia who enjoyed a reputation as 'fruit painters' as well was Joseph Biays Ord (1805-65), son of an ornithologist. He must have been interested in still life as such at an early date, for in 1840 he painted his *Déjeuner à la fourchette*: a work that has nothing in common with the decorative taste of the people who bought fruit pieces for their dining rooms (fig. 53). On a plain table are two oysters, some lemons, biscuits, and a knife, grouped around a decanter and a full wine glass. The light comes from the upper left-hand corner, and the background shows a diagonal division into a bright and a dark area. The fruit and flower paintings of the Peales showed a similar division, but it was a conventional

pattern with them. In Ord's still life the division logically results from the prevailing distribution of light. The whole picture is done in chiaroscuro and a subtle harmony of warm tones prevails. The texture of the objects is illustrated convincingly by purely technical means, the brush strokes being left in their first, vigorous state, in contrast to the smooth and glassy texture of the Peales' paintings. The composition, too, is less regular than those of the previous generation, and although well balanced, its effect is informal. All these characteristics can be summed up in the term 'picturesque.' The painting is realistic, but its realism is fundamentally different from objectivism, for it does not present isolated objects to direct contemplation under the best possible visual conditions. Rather it tends to poetize them by means of suitable lighting and by fusing them into a well-integrated whole in which associations and overtones play an important part. Ord's type of still life is 'one of mood,' to adopt a term from the history of landscape painting, and as such it belongs to the sphere of romantic realism. Its ancestors are the Dutch breakfast pieces of the eighteenth century and the kitchen still lifes of Chardin.

The next step in the stylistic development is represented by the work of a man who, after he had been practically forgotten for more than half a century, was recently called 'perhaps the best still-life painter between the Peales and Harnett, Chase, and Carlsen.' He was Pennsylvania-born John F. Francis (1810-85). From the meager sources available we learn that he lived in Philadelphia and Harrisburg alternately between 1840 and 1855, and afterwards stayed in Wilmington, Delaware. He was known as a portrait and still-life painter. Many of his fruit pieces were sold from the exhibition rooms of the Art Union between 1844 and 1850, but the dates of his still lifes indicate that he continued to paint them in the 'sixties. There is no reason to believe that he was less successful later, even though records of his sales exist only for six years.

The still lifes that he painted as early as the middle of the eighteen fifties show his style fully developed— a style which, seen in the perspective of history, gives Francis a place among the most advanced painters of his period. Two of his important early paintings are in the Prew Savoy collection in Washington, D. C. One of them is signed and dated 1854, but the other lacks a date. The first shows a basket with apples and chestnuts, a porcelain pitcher, glasses, and a dish with apples (fig. 56)—objects repeated almost piece by piece in a painting of the Karolik Collection that bears the date 1859 and is painted in a slightly more fluid manner. Since the second of the pictures in the Prew Savoy Collection, a table piece, shows even more rigidity, I suggest that it be dated before 1854 (fig. 54). An 'epergne' with assorted fruits (grapes, raisins, almonds, and oranges) forms the center of a formal composition in which the elements are wine bottles, with red and white wine glasses, a pitcher of the same type as those in the other two paintings, a plate with a large slice of cheese, oyster crackers, and a silver knife. The ornaments of the pitcher are blue, tinted with gold. A white tablecloth is contrasted with a plain dark background. Evidently the picture was intended to decorate a dining room, but by the keenness of his observation the painter made the conventional subject matter an exquisite visual experience. The champagne glasses, which alternate with small chalices, form a rhythmic pattern around the *basso continuo* of the majestic bowl of fruits. The dark bottles and the bright jar are a minor and a major chord, and only an asymmetrical water glass to the right suggests somewhat roguishly that the whole thing is not quite as solemn as it seems. The glass is, so to speak, a coda, an affix to the score.

Another still life, with a white pitcher, three water glasses, oyster crackers, chestnuts, and apples, the slightly more relaxed style of which suggests the early 'fifties as its date, supplements the stiff orchestra piece with a bit of lighter vocal music (fig. 55). No dignified bowl of fruits prevents the glasses from establishing themselves as an improvised chime, and everything else cheerfully contributes its own voice to an extemporaneous bit of community singing. The still life in the Karolik Collection that is signed and dated 1859 may serve as a striking example of Francis' style in the years before the Civil War. On a table laid with a white cloth is an overturned basket with apples and chestnuts. A piece of cloth is folded backwards covering the basket, and apples and chestnuts are spread over the table. A plate with a sliced apple and a knife, an earthenware jar, and two glasses filled with wine are distributed over the rest of the table. The left side of the background is almost black, the right side somewhat brighter. The light comes from the right and brings out the form of every object with great clarity. Whereas the table in all but a few of Raphaelle Peale's still lifes was placed parallel to the border of the picture, here it is seen from the side so that its borders form oblique angles with the frame. The last vestiges of regularity have vanished from the composition. The 'stable equilibrium' prevailing hitherto has definitely given way to an 'unstable equilibrium' in which a complex relationship is established between the single elements. The painter achieves the precarious balance of his composition by constructing a design of the patterns formed by shadows in contrast to the lighted areas. A highly unconventional use of

pure color complements the bold innovations of the composition. Francis' colors are neither the local colors of the Peales nor the tonal values of an Ord. They rather reflect a study of relative values suggested by the combination of objects of different color and texture. As a result, novel shades of pink, blue, green, and yellow determine the effect of Francis' mature paintings. Evidently the interest in texture is subordinated to the study of volumes and colors under a given light —a principle that in the sphere of the great art of the world was suggested by the landscapes of Corot's Italian period and was not carried through to its last consequences until later on in Cézanne's work. Some anonymous Mexican still lifes in Roberto Montenegro's collection dating from about 1840 display similar tendencies on a more primitive level.

The post-Civil War period of Francis is characterized by a softening of his approach, by an increased freedom of his handwriting and—probably rather late in his life—by a turn from pure artistic research toward a more conventional decorative style. A little still life with cheese and crackers in the Museum of Historic Art in Princeton initialed and dated 1866 (fig. 57) shows Francis' new style in the making: the forms are softer, the brushwork is more impulsive and the composition is tighter.

An overturned basket forms the main motif of a still life with cherries (fig. 58), in which the glassy skin of the fruits is more emphasized than their spherical shape. It was painted in the same year as the Princeton picture. Now emphasis is laid on atmosphere, and the painter seems to have lost some of his interest in volumes. Also that year Francis painted a still life with oranges, raisins, and nuts, in which texture is studied as well as relief (fig. 59). Chiaroscuro unifies the painting, and the colors are correspondingly more subtly blended.

Yet another still life by Francis comes closer to the lavish taste of the post-Civil War period (fig. 60). It shows a fruit basket in the midst of sliced watermelons on a table set up in an Italianate porch with an evening landscape as background. Its composition is more involved and less lucid than in Francis' other paintings, but color and technique are lively. It is reasonable to assume that the still life with evening landscape is a late work of the painter, probably one produced around 1870. It has a charm of its own, though aesthetically it shows the influence of what we used to call the Victorian period. This term really is equivalent to 'post-romanticism,' since it is not restricted to England, but designates a stage of development in which the tenets of the romanticists became common property. This development, like many similar ones, included an element of vulgarization and at the same time indicated that romanticism was no longer creative—creative energies had been directed toward other objectives. The nature of post-romantic art, furthermore, was determined by the character of the society of the second half of the nineteenth century. This character was typically bourgeois.

An uninhibited display of wealth wrought havoc with tact and taste and the emotional quality which was at the core of the Romantic movement survived in a distorted form. That everything good in art was produced in a heartbreaking struggle against society is illustrated in the story of the French impressionists or in the history of the Arts and Crafts Movement in England. A painting by James Welles Champney strikingly illustrates the situation, and has special importance for the study of American still-life painting in the 'seventies and 'eighties. It is called *The Wedding Gifts* and allegedly shows the family of the noted journalist Horace Greeley inspecting an exhibition of presents on a table (fig. 65).

Champney was born in Boston in 1843 and acquired the training of an European *genre* painter in Paris and Antwerp in the 'sixties. He signed his early pictures Champ to avoid confusion with other Boston artists of the same name. Champney was probably unaware that a new art, impressionism, was being born outside the limelight of the Grand Salon in Paris, which dominated international art life. He practiced his art to the delight of his American patrons until his death in 1903 in New York.

All the sham and splendor of the post-romantic era are assembled in the still life of Greeley's table; the figures add importance to the value of the gifts by their admiration of them. From the bottom of a candlestick, which has taken the form of a dragon so that it can be held by the tail, to the ubiquitous 'epergne,' the eye takes in a chaotic array of inane and pretentious objects. The composition does not show the controlled informality of a Francis. The picture is split into unorganized details that try to catch the eye through technical perfection in the painting of textures. The painter is very skilful, but all the expenditure of skill serves a nonartistic purpose: to tell a sentimental story in an engaging manner.

It is in the light of what this picture reveals that we have to analyze the development of still life following the Civil War in America. Disregarding the mass of dull and vulgar still lifes, which were produced in ever-increasing numbers, we discover some American painters in whose work the genuine values of the earlier periods survived the change of taste. The degree to which these artists were influenced by post-romanticism de-

pended on the amount of freedom that individual painters achieved, limited as they were by dependence upon the paying public.

It was the heyday of the Bohème, with life a precarious gamble, that established the artist as a cynic in a marginal sphere of society. Bohemianism in reality lacked most of the glamor of Murger's famous novel that gave it a name. A German Bohemian artist, Severin Roesen, appeared on the American scene some time after the middle of the century. The exact date is not known. A porcelain painter Severin Roesen of Cologne in 1847 exhibited a flower piece and soon disappeared from sight. Whether the American immigrant was the same person cannot be established with certainty. Severin is a common name in Cologne, since St. Severin is a popular saint there. Roesen made his way from New York to Pennsylvania, evidently attracted by the presence of many of his countrymen there. His paintings are scattered along the main highway to the Susquehanna Valley and up the valley to Williamsport, where he finally established himself around 1860. He made his living as a flower painter and occasionally taught art, but alcoholism, the sinister concomitant of the free and easy Bohème, gradually got the better of him. He became socially impossible and with his talent ruined, disappeared in the late 'seventies to die, as rumor has it, in a Philadelphia poorhouse.

The quality of his work is uneven as a result of his drinking habits but in his best works he displayed what Cézanne called the power of 'realization.' He received numerous commissions for large pictures, usually in pairs, of fruit and flowers (figs. 63 and 64). These paintings show the qualities of Roesen's work most convincingly and definitely betray his European training. The tradition of the late Baroque flower painters shows through the surface taste of his time; they recall especially Abraham Mignon. The taste of his own time expresses itself in a somewhat scorched coloration and a materialistic conception: the fruits and flowers seem to be picked and displayed with the salesmanship of a successful grocer. Roesen's still lifes look as if they were show windows full of glamorous, appetizing samples. In fact, it is the show window that forms the model of his compositions in contradistinction to the garden grotto that inspired Mignon and other old Dutch fruit and flower painters. A man in reduced circumstances, so to speak, Roesen looked at the 'good earth's' tantalizing display of fruit only through the glass pane of a show case.

In a monumental still life called *Nature's Bounty*, probably painted between 1860 and 1870 (fig. 62), Roesen seems to sum up his artistic credo. An abundance of luscious fruits is distributed over two super-imposed marble slabs, typical of a window display. Without scruple the painter has placed his glorified show window in a romantic landscape. The left side of the landscape is formed by a dense grove featuring one of the little altars that was a favorite motif of early nineteenth-century landscape architects. A dark grove serves to set off the lighted side of the painting. On the right side a bright but cloudy evening sky contrasts with the darker side of the picture. This device recalls the conventionalized chiaroscuro backgrounds that the Peales employed in their work. When all is said, Roesen's work does not fit badly into the 'Philadelphia School.'

Nature's Bounty was exhibited for the first time after its rediscovery in 1932, and its painter remained unknown until the canvas had been cleaned. The signature was then discovered; it is formed by a tendril originating at the stem of the vine between the marble slabs. Roesen often signed his works in this capricious way. This quaint habit is not without significance, since further study of the picture reveals the spirals and kinks of the tendrils playing a meaningful part in the inventory of his motifs. In his flower painting (fig. 64) the thorny stems of the roses caught his attention. The tendency towards a 'calligraphic' linear style links Roesen with the romanticists of his homeland.

Roesen was the outsider among the still-life painters of the post-romantic period. On the other hand George R. Hall (1825-1913), who painted *genre* pictures as well as still lifes, swam happily with the stream. A man of the world, he studied in Düsseldorf and Paris from 1849 to 1852. He brought home a smooth and efficient technique and success seemed to favor him. The National Academy of Design soon elected him to membership and he became a public favorite. Travels to Italy, Spain, and Egypt found him searching for 'paintable' motifs. The slick scenes he painted from his observations in these countries belong to the irreparably dated artistic sphere of his fellow countryman Champ-ney. Hall's still lifes, in contrast to his landscapes, have an enduring quality apart from their charm as period pieces. In 1871 he painted a still life called *Holly* (fig. 66). On a table parallel to the picture plane, two bowls of fruit, a bottle of liqueur, a wine glass, a partly peeled lemon, a camellia and other objects are grouped in pyramidal arrangement. This is topped by a twig of holly placed horizontally on two differently shaped vessels. The composition would not be greatly different from that of James Peale, except that Peale strove for the clarity of a botanical illustration, whereas Hall does everything to obliterate the geometrical character of arrangement and to stress subjectivity. The carved front edge of the table is overlapped by camellia leaves and lemon skin. Instead of Peale's linear style, a heritage from classicism, Hall shares the tonal attitude of his contemporaries. In this tonal composition chiaroscuro prevails, serving to fuse the parts into a picturesque visual experience. In contradistinction to Roesen, Hall is not interested in the pattern of his models, but primarily in their texture. In each of Roesen's indoor still lifes, bare foreground walls define the still life as a structure, limited to a tier, but Hall looks at a still life as a part of the room. Thus he explains the still life's relation to the space around it by representing the rear wall in complete detail. An open window leads the eye to the horizon, adding a finishing touch of atmospheric treatment.

The painting arouses comfortable associations of well-being and home life, rather than satisfies purely artistic demands. The holly, so conspicuously arranged to catch the eye, and the winter landscape outside the house provide the appealing overtones of a typical Christmas picture. Evidently the artist is striving to please his public simply by displaying motifs that are obvious, familiar, and sentimental instead of selecting and arranging them for deeper aesthetic reasons—a sign that the romantic spirit was rapidly disintegrating into a polite intellectual parlor game.

V. THE STYLE OF TROMPE L'OEIL

ROMANTICISM in one form or another was the leading influence in American art from Washington Allston to the latest representatives of the Hudson River School, but the persistence of the Peale tradition and the best work of the period demonstrates that romanticism was not the only school with important artistic values.

James Peale's objectivism corresponds to the survival of eighteenth-century rationalism; and the primitives represent the survival of the craftsman's spirit in a young, not fully industrialized society. Still another group of painters produced an important body of work, which demands examination on its own terms, for it is distinguished by what may be called 'heightened' realism.

As early as 1823, Raphaelle Peale's *After the Bath* showed a marked tendency to revive the *trompe l'œil*. In the foreground a towel is thrown into relief to produce a tangible quality. However, Raphaelle Peale was not the only painter in America who clung to the tradition of the *trompe l'œil* after it had been abandoned in Europe. In fact, an undercurrent of *trompe l'œil* painting can be traced all through the second quarter of the nineteenth century. This current eventually broadened and progressed from a latent to a manifest role in the second half of the century, transcending the doctrinal character of its beginnings. The result was an illusionistic art that applied the heightened realism of the *trompe l'œil* to still-life motifs generally.

An anonymous *trompe l'œil* dating from 1827 has been attributed to an otherwise unknown painter, Nathaniel Peck, on the basis of the address of a letter seen in the picture (fig. 67). The painting was found in Flushing, New York, and probably is of local origin. This is most astonishing, since the picture is a reinterpretation of Vaillant's *Letter Rack* (fig. 3), and would imply that a painter in a small community outside of New York was familiar with the work of a seventeenth-century Flemish painter. However, since *trompe l'œils* had been popular with European painters all through the eighteenth century, it is reasonable to assume that this letter-rack type was familiar to American painters early in the nineteenth century through copies and reproductions. Nathaniel Peck's version differs from the European because of a strange peculiarity: an eye like those seen in ritual decorations of Freemasons is painted on the letter rack. This motif suggested to its rediscoverers the name, *The All-Seeing Eye*.

In the picture two letters and some printed matter, a folder with cigars, a bow, a vial, a coin, and two keys are tied to the wall by a tape. The letters are addressed to people in New York and Flushing, where Peck resided. The printed matter consists of a New York newspaper, a booklet on what seems to be crystal gazing; and an almanac of the popular variety known for its astrological information. The painting technique is illusionistic, but not subtle. It suggests the amateurishly trained rather than a professional painter as its author. Nothing is known of the artist except his name. He seems to have been interested in abstruse sciences, and to have intended, with the combination of heterogeneous objects with the eye of God in *trompe l'œil*, to convey the feeling that even the most humble object has a transcendental significance. It will be recalled that the German mystic Jacob Boehme, a shoemaker by profession, experienced his spiritual illumination by looking into a glass ball. In the old workshop of his trade, the ball served to concentrate light on tools.

Three years after *The All-Seeing Eye* was painted, a young portrait painter, Charles B. King, painted a *trompe l'œil* known under the title of *Vanity of an Artist's Dream* (fig. 69). King was born in Newport, Rhode Island, in 1785 or 1786 and was one of the last students of Benjamin West in London. He became a successful portrait painter in Washington, D. C., where he died in 1862. Between his stay in London and his Washington years, he lived in Philadelphia for a while, at the time Raphaelle and James Peale were developing their still-life style. This 'Vanitas' is a still life representing the contents of a poor painter's studio piled in a cupboard. The wooden frame of the cupboard runs parallel to the picture frame. This device was used as early as the seventeenth century by such *trompe l'œil* painters as Gysbrecht and was continued into the eighteenth century by Oudry (fig. 6). Among the objects to be seen besides the palette and brushes of the painter are books and letters, and a dish with a piece of bread on it. The books have such significant titles as 'Pleasures of Hope' and 'Pleasures of Imagination.' The broken head of a Greek bust seems to look with empty eyes into the infinite, and in a relief that is part of the contents of the cupboard, an *Abundantia* empties her cornucopia. To the frame is fixed a sheriff's sale list, every line of which is legible, and the text is written with sardonic humor.

The style of the painting is vigorous and displays an efficient use of chiaroscuro. During King's London years he evidently investigated the exhibitions and galleries of the English capital thoroughly and became imbued with the tradition of the Old Masters. It is known that from youth he was conspicuously sober and industrious, and that late in life he attained a notable success as a portrait painter in Washington.

Although his *Vanity of an Artist's Dream* bitterly complains about the callousness of the world towards the aspirations of the artist, King himself could not complain about neglect. He chose the soft way of compromise. This painting indicates that an inner struggle preceded his relinquishing a claim to immortality. In an hour of bitter disillusionment he may have remembered one of the *trompe l'œil* versions of the 'Vanitas' theme in European collections and have given vent to his feelings, adding an element of irony to the conception that was originally unmitigated gloom. The *trompe l'œil* technique gave adequate overtones of intense realism to his pictorial satire.

About twenty years after Nathaniel Peck painted *The All-Seeing Eye*, a draftsman in a Washington government office by the name of Goldsborough Bruff revived the letter-rack type of *trompe l'œil* in a water color (fig. 70). Bruff was born in 1804 and died in 1889, a local celebrity. His lifelong, rather inconspicuous activity at the drawing board was interrupted in 1849 for the two years that he spent in California as leader of a mining expedition. Bruff was a trustee and incorporator of the National Gallery and Art School, established in 1860 by an act of Congress. Although

somewhat erratic and amateurish, he was a man of courage and keen observation.

Goldsborough Bruff's *trompe l'œil* shows an assortment of prints and drawings. As such it recalls a famous *trompe l'œil* by Boilly. It is, however, not a framed picture like Boilly's painting, but one mounted on a board. The outside edges of the paper are painted to resemble the cross section of the board on which cards, letters, drawings, and prints are placed. The assorted papers attest to Goldsborough Bruff's activities as a cartographer, illustrator, designer of coats of arms and ornaments. The letters, part of the pile, are addressed to the artist. They do not show postage stamps. Thus, the picture cannot be dated later than 1847, when the postage stamp was introduced in America. Its style, on the other hand, suggests that it was not painted much earlier, perhaps about 1845.

A business card is among the prints, and is half covered by another sheet of paper. The spectator's curiosity is stimulated by this trick. The 'business,' however, is not taken too seriously, as is shown by a painter's caricature included in the motley arrangement.

We learn from Goldsborough Bruff's posthumous papers that the versatile artist collected coins and scientific curios and wrote about them. The implications of this are interesting, for the development of the *trompe l'œil* in the seventeenth century, we have seen, was closely connected with the establishment of the curio cabinet.

In each of these three examples of American *trompe l'œil* the heightened realism was made to serve as the special objective of the painter. Nathaniel Peck expressed his erratic mysticism when he showed the eye of God watching over his odd collection of insignificant items. Charles B. King conjured up the memory of monastic meditations on the futility of life in order to dramatize the plight of the artist. Goldsborough Bruff advertised his diverse skills in a capricious form suggesting a bizarre personality.

During the second half of the nineteenth century the strain of irrationalism, which never quite disappeared, changed its direction. During the reign of Romanticism it was introspective, but during the heyday of science it became extrovert. Man, in search of the mysterious, no longer looked into himself, but outside, into nature. Of course, he must not look at the familiar nature outside his window, but at an exotic scene. The quest for miracles in the age of the railway led to the search for what in popular travelogues was called 'the wonders of nature.' The plain and matter-of-fact interest in nature that prevailed in the times of old Charles Willson Peale had given way to an enthusiastic curiosity.

The explorer was the hero of the day. The new type of the traveler-painter appeared, the globe-trotter with the paint box who flooded the exhibitions with glamorized views of Egypt and the tropics. These views appealed to the popular interest in science. The interest was somewhat vague and not altogether discriminating, but it did foster serious belief in educational values—a belief that prevented people from accepting the trivial as entertainment. At its best, the body of painting produced to capitalize on this interest fell far short of perfection, but succeeded in communicating the enthusiasm of the sensitive traveler to the spectator by a kind of humanized photography, as in the topographic landscapes of Frederick Edwin Church.

Whereas Church indulged in ambitious panoramas, his contemporary Martin Johnson Heade went in quest of the minute. This painter was a traveler by nature. He was born in 1819 at Lumberville, Bucks County, Pennsylvania, and thus grew up in the orbit of the Philadelphia School. In fact, he lived in Philadelphia for a while as an adult. Not only did he study in Rome and visit England and France, but he also visited South America in 1864 and afterward; and inside the United States he lived in New York, Philadelphia, Boston, Providence, and Trenton. The painter traveled several times in South America before he definitely settled in the United States. He made a trip to Brazil to study the hummingbirds of South America in order to supply materials for illustrating a book planned by a missionary and amateur naturalist, James Cooley Fletcher. Technical difficulties in the reproduction of Heade's miniaturelike paintings are said to have prevented publications of the work. Heade exhibited the originals later on, and sold them to Sir Morton Peto, an English economist. He also painted landscapes, which at their worst derived a cheap success from glowing sunsets, but at their best showed convincing force in interpreting, for example, the atmospheric drama of a storm. In his rare flower pieces (fig. 71) he achieved a new kind of puritan beauty by an intensified realism and a composition close to that of the trompe l'œil. Although highly appreciated during his prime, Heade dropped out of sight even before he died in St. Augustine, Florida, at the age of eighty-four.

The Brazilian studies doubtless are the best of Heade's artistic work. They are close-ups illustrating the life of the bizarre little birds he observed, and of the exotic plant life of their habitat (fig. 72). The fragile petals of the magnificent orchids, the scintillating plumage of the hummingbirds that his eye catches in flight with an uncanny skill—all are rendered with a technique delicate enough for miniature work. And he provides the whole with an almost equally precise landscape background: he traces the rugged branches of giant trees weighed down with flying moss; he counts the leaves of palm trees in their luscious groves; and he indicates every strain of the silvery water in a far-away cascade, while a cloudy sky unfolds a subtle play of light and shadow, color and gray, under his smooth though somewhat pedantic brush.

The chief subject matter of Heade's paintings, the birds and the plants in which he was especially interested, is arranged in a plane parallel to the picture plane, a composition often emphasized by branches forming a kind of trellis. Moreover, these foreground motifs are focused separately and are portrayed with an intensified realism. In this respect Heade's Brazilian pictures are linked with the tradition of the trompe l'œil, although not trompe l'œils in a literal sense. His passionate interest in nature as a scientific phenomenon must have inspired him to develop his individual variety of illusionism as a medium for the student of natural history. Heade's unassuming little paintings have the fascinating aroma of adventure, of discovery, of an exotic world that is also real and mysterious.

The interest in the minute that prompted Heade's studies in foreign countries was shared by a group of painters who rarely moved outside the sheltered world of their studios. It was the development of photography that made people increasingly conscious of detail in the second half of the nineteenth century. The painters first welcomed the new invention as a tool that would enrich their visual experience, but they were soon to learn that it had deprived them of their most reliable source of income, the portrait. Furthermore, it confused the aesthetic issue for many painters, who were naively impressed by the perfection of the camera. Only those painters who represented the tradition of the trompe l'œil did not suffer from the influence of photography; their method had enough in common with photography for them to compete with it.

The painting Locomotive Entering Yard at Night, the work of an unknown artist, introduces a new subject into American painting—machinery (fig. 75). It is a close-up, seen from the engineer's cab. In a slender frame with an arched top, the body of the engine appears in a sharply foreshortened aspect, depicted with the precision of a mechanical draftsman. The silhouette of the frame suggests the arched window of the cab of an old-fashioned locomotive; two such windows appear on each side of the boiler. Our imagination complements the window frame which, if illustrated, would be parallel to the picture plane like the cupboard frames of Gysbrecht, Oudry, and King. It is

[29]

especially this device that links the *Locomotive at Night* with *trompe l'œil* painting. Moreover, the painter emphasized the parts of the engine that are planes and appear parallel to the picture plane. Thus he gave the locomotive an almost tangible reality.

The design of the engine is typical of the early stage of technology, which was afraid of functional forms and as a result prettified machinery by decorating, in this case, the smokestack with classic moldings and by topping valves and pipe ends with neatly polished brass balls. From the lantern on top of the boiler, beams of light reach along the rails into the night, while a lighted train approaches from the background. Dim lights and a blurred contour suggest a freight yard. A few stars show in the sky.

The painting is done in a smooth and somewhat dry technique. The type of the engine as well as the handling of color suggests a date around 1880—in its period a unique achievement. Turner had discovered the railway as a pictorial motif as early as 1844, and Monet had just painted his *Gare St.-Lazare* (1877). The English romanticist had reduced the train in his famous *Rain, Steam and Speed* to a fleeting vision, and the French impressionist had studied the effect of light on the new world of steel, glass, and smoke; the anonymous American—a superrealist by intuition—painted the engine for its own sake. He painted, to all practical purposes, a still life in motion.

The unknown artist to whom we owe this fascinating little work was assuredly no primitive, for he had mastered perspective and showed a skilled hand in the representation of engine parts. He knew how to suggest the mood of the night scenery, and must have been thoroughly familiar with his subject. Is it not probable that the painter was an engineer, enthusiastic about the railroad and acquainted with the technical drawing of railway equipment? If so, this painting was undertaken as a more personal project in visual representation than his daily work at the drawing board required.

There are isolated instances of artistic ventures that moved in a similar direction at about the same time, including a still life by an otherwise forgotten painter, Morston Constantine Ream, who lived from 1840 to 1898 and was active in New York. It is dated 1877 and shows a plum, a small wineglass, nuts and a fly on a table covered with a white cloth (fig. 74). The background is plain and shows the familiar diagonal division in light and shadow. One of the walnuts is cracked, and part of its kernel is on the table. The work is painted with almost painful attention to detail. The fruits and the insect are larger than natural scale, and this together with the exactitude of the representation

endows the whole with a slightly uncanny overtone: the magnified fly looks dangerous, and the bulges of the kernel induce a morbid anatomical effect. It is as if the painter had discovered in the commonplace a mysterious quality resulting from the intensity of the feeling it aroused in him. In his desire to express the depth of this experience, he resorted to the device of enlarging the objects in the immediate foreground.

The 'magic' effect, which in Morston Ream's picture is limited by a somewhat amateurish technique, was developed into a sophisticated style by a highly competent artist, William M. Harnett. Born in Clonakilty, County Cork, Ireland, in 1848, Harnett was brought to the United States by his parents when he was only a year old. The family settled in Philadelphia, where the father died after a few years and left his family in dire poverty. When William was seventeen, he learned the trade of an engraver, and at nineteen he received his first training in art at the Pennsylvania Academy of Fine Arts in Philadelphia. Two years later he moved to New York, and continued his studies in evening classes, and for a short time under a private teacher, Thomas Jensen. About 1870 he began to exhibit his paintings at the National Academy of Design. He sold his work at modest prices, up to $150 a painting, and won friends among the collectors. In 1875 he gave up engraving definitely and returned to Philadelphia, exhibiting there at the Academy. In 1878 he left for Europe, stayed first in London and after a few months moved to Frankfort-on-the-Main, where he lived in the house of his patron, a German collector, for the next two years. From 1882 to 1884 he worked in Munich and traveled through Germany, collecting 'paintable' antiques for his studio.

His pictures were eagerly sought after, but the academic pundits whom he approached for instruction repudiated his work. As a result he gave up studying with teachers and preferred to go to the Old Masters in quest of instruction. A strong 'elective affinity' drew him to the *trompe l'œil* painters and to those Dutch and Flemish still-life painters of the seventeenth century whose realism came close to the *trompe l'œil*.

By 1884 he felt that he could make a bid for world renown: from Paris he sent an elaborate still life to the Grand Salon, the undisputed court where the struggle for international recognition was decided. Every year during the 'eighties, a small volume appeared in Paris in which a selection of forty paintings from the Grand Salon were reproduced and discussed. Author of the volume was Louis Enault, a former royalist, exile, globe-trotter, and novelist forgotten today, but whose books were widely read in his time and whose art criticism was considered authoritative in the *grand monde*. Enault's selection of what he dubbed the best paintings of the year was accepted abroad the more readily because it excluded everything 'controversial.' Turning the pages of the volume of his *Paris Salons* that contains the harvest of 1885, one is surprised to find not one of the masters who today make the glory of French nineteenth-century painting. Sugary *genre* paintings and pretentious historic compositions prevail. Some of the unobtrusive landscapes are the least offensive. In this questionable company appears Harnett's *Trophée de Chasse* (now in the Columbus Gallery of Fine Arts, Columbus, Ohio). It is interesting to read Enault's comment. The inclusion of this foreign work seems to have shattered the wall of conventions that otherwise made the verdicts of this sham expert a mockery of art criticism, for on Harnett's painting he wrote some lines of truly understanding appraisal: 'J'ai rarement vu un relief plus puissant . . . une vigueur arrivant au trompe l'œil. Il serait vraiment difficile de mieux faire.' Whatever Enault's criticism was worth, it was considered authoritative by the public, and Harnett profited by it. He returned to America in 1886 and settled in New York, a man whose fortune was made. His prices gradually rose to $2000 and perhaps even more, but he did not enjoy his success for long. A rheumatic disease from which he vainly sought relief in European and American health resorts seems to have undermined his resistance, and an illness of a few days caused his death in 1892. For a short time his paintings were sought after eagerly and some of them sold for as much as $10,000, but forty years later, dusty and blunted, they stood in attics and secondhand shops, entirely forgotten. An art dealer in New York rediscovered Harnett and exhibited his work in 1939. This exhibition was a sensational success, and since then collectors and museums have vied with each other to secure his paintings.

A fascinating story—and one that forcefully raises the questions: What made Harnett's work so quickly famous and equally quickly forgotten, and what is the reason for its resurgence? Why has it escaped the fate of the other works that won fame side by side with it in the Paris Salon, the fate of being dated beyond salvation?

Harnett was a still-life painter to the exclusion of everything else. According to his own words he did only two portraits in his whole life. There is an early painting by Harnett called *To the Opera*, a close-up of a hand carrying a walking stick (fig. 76)—a bizarre little work that in a roundabout way seems to disclose a negative attitude toward men, for it substitutes a limb for the whole figure. Not satisfied with that, the painter gave the hand a macabre, lifeless appearance. It hints

that he fought shy of people and was haunted by the thought of death. . . There are reasons that make this interpretation at least worth considering: Harnett avoided publicity whenever possible, he disliked portrait painting, and he was a sick man.

Practically all that we know about him is based on two meager sources: an interview that he gave at the height of his fame, and an obituary in a periodical. In his interview he carefully avoided giving anything more personal than some anecdotes and a few hints about his technique. The obituary was written by a friend of his who supplied valuable biographical data but evidently was not equipped to discuss art. It is worth noticing that the magazine that published the obituary was *The American Catholic Historical Researches*. This magazine was interested in Harnett primarily as a famous representative of Catholic culture. The fact that the obituary appeared in a periodical devoted to the history of the Church suggests that Harnett was a religious-minded man. This certainly is not unimportant, but for Harnett's personality his paintings are our main source of information—and it seems that they draw the veil even more tightly over the artist's self, for they present themselves as cool and detached illustrations of commonplace objects; when they tell a story it is a painfully banal one. It is a striking paradox that in spite of his trite subject matter, the effect of Harnett's work is esoteric and almost mysterious.

On a small canvas dated 1870 and called *Raspberries and Ice Cream* (fig. 77), Harnett displayed all the main qualities of his later works. On a carved table with a marble top a strangely naked-looking metal bowl holds the berries. A dish of pinkish ice cream is to the left, with a spoon sticking in the fluffy matter like a dagger. Another dish with a piece of yellowish cake is directly in front of the bowl, and dark grapes are in the foreground. The ubiquitous drop of water on the grapes—a Dutch heritage—is not missing. The style is crisp; the colors pink, yellow, white, brown, and purple clash in a way that is utterly foreign to the prevailing taste for the 'gold tone' of the galleries. A picture like this was indeed rare at the time. The painter must have possessed deep-rooted inhibitions, which prevented him from falling into the many traps of the post-romantic period. There is something austere and clean about the group of Harnett's paintings to which the ice cream still life belongs and that originated in the first half of the 'seventies. Most of these still lifes display solidly bound volumes, letters, money bills, coins, conical inkwells, goose quills and other objects pertaining to the world of the office. The volumes are gazetteers, or as we would call them, business directories. Harnett never tired of depicting these objects in varied combinations that demonstrate the different artistic potentialities offered by a limited number of insignificant things. Although not *trompe l'œils*, these paintings display a markedly intensified realism. Form and texture are depicted with an unerring and sensitive hand. The color scheme is deeply warm with rich grays and areas of almost luminous red or blue. Occasionally some fruits appear in the composition, but they are not allowed to exhibit their juicy life energy: they are nearly petrified, caged into an ugly wooden basket to be sold at the market (fig. 79) or laid out isolated as on the shelf of a thrifty spinster (fig. 82). Nevertheless, these paintings have an inner strength that impresses itself on the spectator. Whether consciously or unconsciously, the painter is grappling in these works with fundamental problems of composition. He interprets the world in terms of a solid geometry that on a more pedestrian basis recalls Raphaelle Peale.

It is not accidental that the words 'austere,' 'thrifty,' and 'pedestrian' offer themselves as most suitable for characterizing Harnett's paintings discussed so far—directly or indirectly, they are related to commercial value (fig. 78). Either they belong to the hard and sober world of the banker (and one could easily imagine that Dickens' Mr. Scrooge would have been delighted with them), or they reduce organic nature to the rank of a commodity (fig. 80). One would not be surprised to see a price tag fastened to the stale cantaloupe, the wormeaten apple, the tiny grape and the lonely plum in his fruit piece of 1877 (fig. 82). What a distance between the parsimonious Harnett and the wastrel Roesen, who in *Nature's Bounty* exalted the abundance of the good earth! Harnett showed himself fascinated by the cold paraphernalia of capitalism. It is true, however, that Harnett achieved a solidity and clarity of form foreign to Roesen.

Apart from paintings distinguished by their strictly structural conception, Harnett painted a group of pictures in the 'seventies in which texture rather than form was emphasized. These paintings show beer mugs, tobacco pipes, and newspapers, arrayed in a way that looks casual but that is really the result of careful planning. I should like to call the group 'bachelor still lifes'—an expression which, in a certain sense, characterizes Harnett's work in general; for the world of the woman is practically excluded from all of it. In these bachelor still lifes Harnett goes to an extreme in carrying out his desire to characterize textures. He distinguishes the porous earthenware of an unglazed mug from the smooth surface of the meerschaum of the pipe by giving its color a rough, sandlike grain. Though questionable from an aesthetic point of view, this method bestows upon the objects a strangely heightened life. It is worth noticing that Harnett never resorted to this or a similar device when he painted really living things like apples or cantaloupes. On the contrary he rather avoided giving a natural, organic aspect to the fruits he painted. This coincides well with his bias against painting portraits. He shuns real life and prefers to project his own life into dead things.

Most of his still lifes suggest that the owner of the objects had just left the room, after dropping them carelessly on the table. A tobacco pipe is on a folded newspaper; its contents, the half-burned tobacco, are spread on the table; broken matches with blackened ends are strewn about (fig. 81). We observe that some glow is left and is about to burn a hole in the tablecloth, and since the whole picture is painted in a manner akin to that of the *trompe l'œil*, we feel tempted to extinguish the fire. Similarly, we have a tantalizing desire to unfold and read the newspaper, just as in Vaillant's *Letter Rack* we have an urge to investigate the half-opened letters.

The character of this group of pictures, it is true, comes dangerously close to the dull taste of the bourgeoisie of the day, but in the 'eighties Harnett's increased familiarity with the Old Masters—a result of his years of traveling—gave him new impulses that he, a man of strictly descriptive talent, needed in order to create anything new. Because for him creating must have been synonymous with penetrating, his choice of objects and his faithful delineation sheds light on the emotional sources of his artistic inspiration.

Evidently Harnett was influenced by some of the historic types of the *trompe l'œil* found in European galleries. The experiences that prepared him for their digestion was provided by native products—there were enough American still lifes of a *trompe l'œil* character to be known to him at home. These paintings, I have shown, represented some of the main types of the older European *trompe l'œil* in a more or less primitive form. In the European museums, Harnett saw *trompe l'œils* that were not provincial imitations, but genuine masterpieces. Here was the challenge. He began to reinterpret them in the early eighteen eighties. In 1881 he painted *Old Souvenirs*, a free version of Vaillant's *Letter Rack* (figs. 85 and 3). Assembled on a wooden wall are booklets, a newspaper, the photograph of a little girl, some prints, a poster and the ubiquitous letter, which arouses our curiosity but does not give us the full story of the souvenirs. They are his own souvenirs, hinting at the more profound aspects of his thought. The miscellaneous souvenirs on the letter rack conceal rather than disclose the experiences for which they stand, but the fact that the poster in the center advertises fire insurance suggests that 'inside' there is danger of a conflagration. . .

Inside—the word gains a great significance if we examine a group of paintings with their one object in common: a closed door. The door serves as a background for the display of odd objects: dead fowl and game, musical instruments, books, and vessels—all hung on cupboard doors or otherwise placed before the door in an arrangement that seems far fetched. For who would block a door with all these objects or select such a hazardous place for them?

Seen as links in the chain of historical evolution, these paintings by Harnett can be explained as a fusion of two types of *trompe l'œils*: Hondecoeter's dead fowl hanging on a wooden wall and Gysbrecht's cupboard loaded with books and bric-a-brac. But the historical explanation does not tell us why this fusion took place and why in just this way. Harnett's still lifes have a 'brooding quality,' to quote Edgar Preston Richardson's appropriate term. This effect transcends the sense of simple pleasure created by other well-painted still lifes.

To be sure, Harnett always remained fanatically interested in the appearance of things. But he arranged his objects in a paradoxical way, so as to make us wonder whether he really is fascinated more by them or by the unknown things hidden behind the door. Take the *For Sunday Dinner* (1884) as an example: a plucked turkey and a feathered chicken hang from a big nail in a rough plank door fitted with solid iron hinges (fig. 86). An equally solid iron padlock is provided, but the clasp is free and the lock hangs from its chain with the key in the keyhole. The painter emphasizes this state of things by his use of light and shadow. In the painting *The Trophy of the Hunt*, painted a year later, a dead hare is suspended from a nail on a wooden door decorated with large, elaborate wrought-iron hinges (fig. 87). There is no indication that the door is open. It is more solidly built than the first one; but one of the arms of the upper hinge is broken, and a hole shows where it was fastened to the wood with a huge nail. This incongruous motif has a twofold function. The first is obvious: to break the monotony of the pattern; the second is deeper: to negate the effect of solidity that the door displays. It looks as if somebody had tried to break in, but had given up even after the hinge had given way.

In 1892, the year of his death, Harnett painted *The Old Cupboard Door* (fig. 89). The door that gives the picture its title has a big keyhole and massive iron hinges, suggesting that the inside of the cupboard would be inaccessible if the planks of the door were intact. As it is, however, the door has openings large enough to allow a peep inside. A violin with a bow, a bugle with sheet music, and a group consisting of three books, a Dutch earthenware jar, and a sheet of music are arranged in front of the door. One of the books is the *Odyssey*, the other an Italian treatise dated 1507.

These heterogeneous objects are on a single plane—an arrangement which, as I have shown, creates a mysterious impression in a *trompe l'œil*. Here the mystery is deepened because all these objects obstruct the approach to the cupboard. Our attention is divided between the puzzling foreground and the unknown contents of the cupboard behind the broken door.

Harnett said his painting of still life was exclusively a necessity turned into a virtue. According to his own statement, it was poverty that determined his choice of medium and his continuance in it. He could not afford to hire models, so he said. But this explanation is not adequate, for his success was enough to remove all financial difficulties. Moreover, the statement of the artist does not even touch the most striking problem, namely, how he came to be devoted to the device of arranging heterogeneous objects in such a way as to haunt the spectator by their irrational effect.

The titles of Harnett's still lifes, *After a Night's Study*, for instance, or *Mortality and Immortality*, or *Music and Good Luck*, suggest superficial features only: books, a skull, a manuscript, a violin, and a horseshoe. They do not allude to the 'deeper meaning,' to use Panofsky's phrase. We need to know much more than we do about Harnett's life in order to unearth the foundations of his enigmatic work, but we can grasp an occasional hint which, in the light of other clues, gives us something to go on. The slips of paper, for instance, may betray something the painter chose not to reveal directly. If the fire insurance poster really suggests a smoldering desire, the photograph of the little girl might suggest that the actual content of the old souvenir is the restrained lament of a solitary man who longs without hope for the return of a childhood love. One should recall that Harnett was a sick man. Even during his European travels he tried in vain to regain his health in Carlsbad, and with equal futility he visited the Hot Springs of Arkansas. The serious character of this illness is attested by his early death.

Edouard Roditi interpreted Harnett's work as 'necromancy.' Although this term is too romantic, it contains a grain of truth: his paintings are the work of a man who, in the words of the Swiss poet Conrad Ferdinand Meyer, 'kept friends with Death,' who was conscious of his precarious condition and chose renunciation as his answer to a stern fate. Renunciation, moreover, was an answer that accorded with his religion, and it seems that Harnett developed the gentle attitude of a true recluse. Eventually, he might have reasoned, the sinister, cracked door leading to the repressed wishes of his inner self would be definitely sealed, and the artist could content himself with recording the surface of the things that formerly appeared in the enigmatic light of a reverie. This would explain why, aside from his enigmatic compositions, Harnett gradually painted more and more pictures of a plain and obvious type, paintings with a range restricted to an exploration of surface values. *The Faithful Colt* (fig. 84), *The Tobacco Pipe, The Old Violin,* and *Mandolin* (fig. 88) belong to this category. The panel forming the background of the last is in a wall, not a door. An almost identical panel background appears in one of his most ambitious compositions, *Messengers of Peace* (frontispiece), painted in 1890. In this and some other late compositions, one of which he called significantly *My Gems* (1888), Harnett passed in review the models that had formerly been his favorites. In *Messengers of Peace,* we find the old volumes, the Dutch jar, the sheet of music, the folded newspaper, the flute and the candlestick, the tobacco box, and the tobacco pipe that sheds its smoldering ashes ominously on the paper. The artificial arrangement of the still life in *Messengers of Peace* contradicts the fiction kept alive in his bachelor still lifes of the 'seventies that somebody had carelessly dropped his pipe and other things on the table. As a result this beautiful composition lacks something of the inner logic displayed by the informal paintings. The title, finally, does not conceal a deeper meaning, unless we take it as an indication that Harnett had begun to find peace in the mastery of the obvious after he had all but extinguished something more disquieting than the glowing ashes of an overturned tobacco pipe.

According to his own testimony Harnett tried to exaggerate the particular textures of his models: he chose objects in which the character of the texture would appear to best advantage. He said to his interviewer:

In painting from still-life I do not closely imitate nature. Many points I leave out and many I add. Some models are only suggestions. The whole effect of still-life painting comes from its tone, and the nearer one attains perfection, the more realistic the effect will be.

It is significant that the artist strove for a perfection that nature did not offer him, but that he considered this perfection to be identical with realism. Evidently he called realism what we term superrealism: a heightened interpretation of reality expressed by the old technique of the *trompe l'œil.*

The aesthetic element of Harnett's heightened realism has been defined succinctly and comprehensively by Arthur Everett Austin, Jr.:

The eye is enabled to experience in the picture what it is not permitted to do in actuality, that is to focus on a much larger area in complete detail, rather than having to be content to focus on one detail at a time. It is as though one were wearing a wide-angled telescope for glasses or could observe nature always in terms of the sharpened clarity and heightened color of an image thrown on the ground glass finder of a camera.

Austin's analysis recalls the observation that the *trompe l'œil* of the Renaissance and the Baroque periods was closely related to the peep show—a contrivance that in turn is akin to the camera obscura, the prototype of the ground glass finder in photography.

It remains to be explained why Harnett's paintings were so popular with his contemporaries. It has been suggested that his style 'satisfied an obscure idea of perfection,' and this interpretation seems to be corroborated by Harnett's use of the word 'perfection' in his interview. This urge for perfection, it could be argued, appealed to the wealthy patrons of the 'gilded decades' whose materialistic taste valued the perfection of workmanship higher than other qualities in art.

Harnett's preoccupation with money as subject matter for painting actually must have appealed to the *nouveau riche,* although his predilection stemmed from psychological qualities very different from their own. Even as an adolescent in Philadelphia he had entertained members of a reading circle by painting the facsimile of a one-dollar bill on a membership form. In later life he once painted a five-dollar bill for the owner of a popular Philadelphia bar with such success, we are told, that scarcely an evening passed without an attempt on the part of one of the less sober customers to filch the painted paper money. At the instigation of the Treasury Department the painter was arrested and his pictures of paper currency were confiscated. The amusing legal incident ended with Harnett's being released and his paintings returned to him—but not without a warning from the pompous judge to refrain in the future from such suspicious activities.

Whether Harnett was inclined to love money for its own sake—and his pedantic technique as well as the austerity of his style suggests the possibility of such a disposition—whether the poverty of his early years made him money conscious, or whether the one developed from the other, he was certainly no materialist in the manner of the wealthy speculators who built their faked châteaux on Fifth Avenue. He was too sensitive to be greedy, and when he indulged in his weakness for painting dollar bills he always did it with his tongue in his cheek (fig. 83). A gentle self-irony distinguishes these pictures, and this self-irony is part and parcel of his subtle sense of humor, which is to be felt in many significant details of his paintings. This is especially true of his predilection for labels as motifs. He seems to enjoy roguishly making a literal use of the *trompe l'œil*: for example, the label of one of his still lifes showing the display of a secondhand book shop (fig. 90) was painted so true to life that a guard had to be placed before the picture when it was exhibited; for the visitors, believing that a real label was pasted carelessly on the canvas, tried again and again to tear it off.

Despite the superficial appeal that his paintings had for an indiscriminating public, the more refined among his admirers must have felt that there was something more to Harnett's work than trickery. Its emotional overtone could not have failed to strike a sympathetic chord in some beholder. The less obvious the overtone, the more magic the attraction must have been. In the overtone of Harnett's work there is advice, consolation in the face of affliction. Try to derive, he seems to say in a low voice, a gentle pleasure from the humble things of your daily surroundings—give them something of your own life, and they will become friends in your misfortune.

It was the fundamental change of taste at the *fin de siècle* that made Harnett's paintings appear so obsolete as to lose their public altogether, at least temporarily.

Harnett's success brought into being a short-lived school of the style of *trompe l'œil* in America. The members of this group seem to have had patrons in their own time, but they have left no traces in the literature of art. J. Haberle, one of the most gifted of the group, is said to have been active in Connecticut at the end of the last century. The Springfield Museum of Art owns two signed works from his hand: a twenty-dollar bill on dark background, dated 1890 (fig. 93), and a signed but undated painting, *Cigar Box and Pipe* (fig. 94). Both are *trompe l'œils*: the twenty-dollar bill is a *tour de force* of painstaking rendering of details in which the painter goes even farther than Harnett (fig. 91). The *Cigar Box and Pipe* puts Harnett's illusionist technique in the service of an eccentric imagination. In it the picture area is taken up by a board of plywood fastened to a hidden base with screws, one of which is missing, and a tobacco pipe is suspended from a nail

driven into the plywood. A rectangular opening is sawed in the center of the board, and the top of a cigar box is fastened like a picture into the opening by means of a toothpick. All of this is done so carelessly that the 'picture' slants in its 'frame' and shows a triangular slot of darkness. In the top of the cigar box is a hinged flap that can be opened by means of a cord forming a sling. This contrivance suggests the playful tinkering of a boy—children saw holes in cigar box lids and drop marbles through.

The snapshot of a smiling girl holding a cat is fastened to the right of the cigar box, even more carelessly than the top of the cigar box to the board. The little picture shows fissures and cracks, and four matches stick out from behind it. A profile caricature, probably of the painter himself, is carved into the right-hand corner of the picture above the signature, which also is carved into the plywood.

The studied absurdity of the composition approximates the irrational effects introduced some forty years later by the surrealists. The coincidence is more striking than in the work of Harnett, who is said to have anticipated surrealism, although he never consciously strove for irrational effects. The conception of a dark space behind a flimsy surface of commonplace things seems to have haunted Haberle in the same way it haunted Harnett. The photo of the pin-up girl from the gay 'nineties is used to keep some matches ready for the pipe. Hence the photo is cracked. Such bad treatment might suggest that a not too satisfactory experience with some woman was in the back of the painter's mind. To frame as commonplace an object as the top of a cigar box so elaborately is to repudiate the pretension of painting in general, and the depreciatory implication of the arrangement is emphasized by its cheap and makeshift execution.

The painter John F. Peto, in contrast to the whimsical Haberle, was more disposed to rationalize the enigmatic elements in the style of Harnett, who must have been their mutual model. In his *Memories of 1865* (fig. 95) he uses all the devices of Harnett, including the torn labels, to produce a perfect *trompe l'œil*, but for all his effort he conveys only a rather obvious symbolism: above an oval photograph of Abraham Lincoln a hunter's knife is suspended, like the sword of Damocles, and the initials of the president as well as the figures 6 and 5 are carved in the wooden boards which, true to the *trompe l'œil* tradition, form the background of the whole. The composition evidences a subtle sense of design. At the height of Harnett's fame, some of Peto's paintings were sold as works of Harnett. Like Harnett, he was a man of frail health. Born in Florida in 1863, he died in 1914 at Island Heights, New

Jersey, where he had built a studio filled with antiques and bric-a-brac.

In some instances, the allegorical overtone of the type of *trompe l'œil* represented by Peto outweighed the artistic elements, as illustrated in two paintings by otherwise unknown artists named F. Danton, Jr., and W. S. Reynolds. Both pictures date from 1894 and present their titles, *Time is Money* and *Time, Religion and Politics,* on a painted label inside the composition itself (figs. 68 and 92). In Danton's picture, a somewhat summary technique accords with the obviousness of the idea: an alarm clock set at seven o'clock is used as the counterpart of a bundle of five- and ten-dollar bills. The arrangement shows the pattern of a pair of scales with a dollar sign as the center. The nail holes and the keyhole, familiar to us from Harnett, are not missing. Reynolds is more subtle as a painter, and his symbolism shows a certain sense of humor.

The short duration of the vogue of the *trompe l'œil* is demonstrated by the posthumous fate of Richard LaBarre Goodwin, who, at his death in 1910 at Orange, New Jersey, was called in a newspaper obituary 'one of the most famous painters in the country.' With the exception of an inaccurate obituary of a few lines in *Art News,* not a single word seems to have been printed about him in books on art or in art magazines, and he was so completely forgotten when the Museum of Modern Art exhibited one of his paintings in 1939 that except for the obituary in the *Art News,* no biographical data was available for the catalogue. Only the eventual discovery of his death record and two old newspaper clippings shed any light on his life. However provincial he may have been in the eyes of his progressive contemporaries, he outlived the favorites of the art critics of his time.

Richard LaBarre Goodwin was born in 1840 at Albany, New York, the son of a successful portrait and miniature painter, Edwin W. Goodwin. His teachers were three obscure painters, whose names mean nothing to us: LeClear, Jacob, and Hekking. For a number of years he traveled in California, Colorado, and Oregon to study game and landscape. During the Lewis and Clark Exhibition of 1905 in Portland, Oregon, he saw the door of the cabin in which President Theodore Roosevelt stayed as a rancher in South Dakota. This strange exhibit inspired him to a painting originally called *Oregon Game* and later on *Theodore Roosevelt's Cabin Door.* According to the *Portland Oregonian* of 28 April 1907:

The Exposition Management lent him the door, which he took to his studio in the Portland Hotel and painted. He recognized the battered woodwork as an ideal background on which to construct an Oregon game picture. Consulting those interested in sports, he secured the old muzzle-loading fowling piece formerly owned and used by Phil Sheridan. In the upper corner of the picture hangs the Roosevelt soft hat and his dog whistle. Suspended from the center is a string of full plumaged ducks selected from a bag made by the artist in the Columbia slough.

It was proposed that the picture be purchased from the artist and presented to President Roosevelt, the price of $2500 to be subscribed by Oregon residents. At the time of this news article, it was expected that the fund would be raised within a few days, and the plan was to present the painting to the president at Jamestown, Virginia.

From this moment on all trace of the picture was lost. The obituary in *Art News* mentioned it but added that it had been shown in the Portland Exhibition—a mistake caused by the fact that the actual cabin had been shown at the Exhibition. The catalogue of the Museum of Modern Art evidently based its reference to the picture on the obituary. There is, however, a reproduction of LaBarre Goodwin's lost painting in the issue of the *Portland Oregonian,* which contains the description quoted above. This reproduction shows that a painting called *Hunter's Equipment* in the Springfield Museum is all but identical with the lost *Roosevelt's Cabin Door;* in fact, that the Springfield painting is actually a second version of *Roosevelt's Cabin Door* with a pair of boots and a pouch added to the group of the rifle and the ducks (fig. 96). Eventually a third version was identified in a painting by LaBarre Goodwin in the lobby of Hotel Pfister in Milwaukee, there called inconspicuously *Still Life.* It is very similar to the 'lost' first version. Charles Pfister, the late owner of the hotel, acquired it about 1915 from the Henry Reinhardt Art Studios, of Milwaukee.

Attached to the panel of the door is a penny post card addressed to 'Mr. LaBarre Goodwin, Washington, D. C.,' and dated 9 August 1890. The painting itself bears the signature of the painter, with 'Syracuse, New York,' added. The date on the post card has been interpreted erroneously as the date of the picture, which in reality must have been painted between 1905 and the artist's death in 1910. Goodwin used the date 1890, no doubt, to allude in a capricious way to the time when Roosevelt actually slept behind the cabin door of the painting; for in letters to Senator Henry Cabot Lodge, Roosevelt stated that he lived at Elkhorn Ranch in Dakota from 23 September to about 11 October 1890. The painter's use of the wrong month is not surprising, for the inclusion of the card was a whimsical touch, and he doubtless had to rely on inexact sources for his information.

LaBarre Goodwin's painting is the work of an accomplished draftsman who uses the *trompe l'œil* technique to perfection. It lacks the enigmatic overtones of Harnett's best work, but it reveals an unusual understanding of form. Its honesty is disarming, however one might object to its undeniable dryness. And in one direction LaBarre Goodwin outdid Harnett and the rest of the group: he included the picture frame in the composition, as once did Charles Willson Peale in his *Staircase Group*, painting it as if it were the frame of the door itself and providing real hinges and a real lock—a device that apparently took the *trompe l'œil* to its extreme.

But this was not the ultimate in the *trompe l'œil*, as the Bostonian game and sports painter Alexander Pope (1849-1924) was to demonstrate. Pope enjoyed the favor of race-horse fans and dog breeders more than of connoisseurs. He catered to the taste of his wealthy patrons by a faithfulness to nature that was photographic in a stunning but superficial way. He painted *trompe l'œils* of dead birds in a somewhat pedestrian but not unpleasant style (fig. 98)—a style shared with a semi-primitive, the Connecticut painter E. E. Case (Suffield, 1840-1919). Case was superior to him, however, in the matter of taste, as is shown by his *Woodcock* in the museum of Springfield, Massachusetts (fig. 97).

Poor taste was undeniably the chief weakness of the successful Alexander Pope. As a matter of fact, it was the coarseness of his realism that led the *trompe l'œil* ad absurdum in its ultimate stage and that surpassed even LaBarre Goodwin's trick with the door: Pope painted a lion in a cage so true to life that the picture was exhibited behind actual iron bars, an arrangement meant to produce the illusion that there was a real lion in the cage. The painting was exhibited in this fashion at the hall of the Old Plaza Hotel in New York and drew admirers from all over the country. It was imitated even in Salt Lake City. In employing the tricky decoration of hotel lounges, the *trompe l'œil* had reached the apogee of its development.

Painters of a more subtle disposition must have recognized the impass to which unbridled illusionism had led them. At least such seems to have been true of Martin J. Heade. In the 'seventies and 'eighties this restless traveler made a name for himself in the United States as a painter of landscapes with realistic renderings of atmospheric phenomena, especially sunsets and thunderstorms. They are executed in a rather thin technique that reminds one somewhat of the Düsseldorf tradition, but some of them reveal a sensitivity that strikingly transcends the pedantic manner of this school. In one of his best hours Heade painted a view of his studio: a big canvas showing a rivulet winding through a plain is set on trestles, so that we do not see its frame but are made to believe that the landscape really extends indefinitely (fig. 73). The attempt at deceptive realism is carried so far that the water of the rivulet in the picture drips from the canvas to the floor of the studio. In the dark area between the trestles, a strange being, a kind of full moon with a human face and matchlike arms and legs, appears, looking critically at the falling water. It seems probable that the 'gremlin in the studio,' as the picture was named after its recent rediscovery, was suggested to the painter by the circular cross sections of the trestle beams. This is a playful interpretation of accidental form as faces and bodies—a type of interpretation that has given rise to numerous pictorial conceptions, ranging from the 'man in the moon' of the children to the 'double images' of some of the present-day surrealists. Heade's merry conceit, however, has a deeper meaning. The *trompe l'œil* style, once a medium of ideas, had degenerated and outlived itself for the time being. Its best epitaph consequently was irony.

VI. FROM NATURALISM TO IMPRESSIONISM

THE REVIVAL of the style of *trompe l'œil* was not the only development in the history of nineteenth-century art that was exclusively American. The panoramic landscape of the Hudson River School was equally original and had no antecedent or parallel in Europe. The painters of this school strove to represent the large open spaces of America. This task could not be achieved with conventional methods; moreover the American public demanded exactness in the representation of reality. The only device that satisfied both the space-feeling and the desire for precise information was the panorama, a product of applied optics. Actually, there were two kinds of panoramas. The older one, introduced to America about 1815 by Robert Fulton and John Vanderlyn, made use of a circular building, whose inner wall showed a painted view or scene that spectators observed from a platform in the center. Because the field of vision was not limited by a frame, the painting achieved an added naturalness. The second type consisted of a strip of paintings made to pass before the eyes of an audience. It was developed around 1840 in St. Louis by a group of stage painters to create the illusion of a trip made on a steamboat along the Mississippi.

Thomas Cole was the first to apply the teachings of the circular panorama to painting, and created the paroramic style. The technological basis of the panorama and the peep show were similar, for both served to create the illusion of reality. Since the panoramic landscape was derived from the panorama and the *trompe l'œil* from the peep show, each art form has the nature of an optical demonstration. It was this peculiar echo of clever illusionistic techniques that made the panoramic landscape and the *trompe l'œil*

popular in America, for America is the country of documentation.

The Hudson River School, especially in its beginnings, had great charm. True, the technique of the school was not strong even at the outset, but the best paintings of the group had a touch of the atmosphere of Turner. Later on, the interest of the painters was mainly topographical, and the laying on of colors became mechanical, the draftsmanship pedantic. This degeneration of skill, however, was not limited to the panoramic painters. After the middle of the nineteenth century America lost contact with the creative elements in European art. A time lag developed, and American art became antiquated and provincial. The atmospheric problems with which the Hudson River painters struggled could not be solved in a way satisfactory to the modern eye; the European innovations, naturalism and impressionism, had to be assimilated before the art of America could speak the language of its own time.

This is no less true of the still life than of the landscape, though in a modified sense. The still-life painter was less concerned with atmosphere than with texture, and the experiments of the post-impressionists had to be studied before a new variety of 'heightened realism' could be developed to match the harder outlines of modern America.

Like the botanic-decorative school of fruit and flower painters, naturalism and impressionism originated in France; but the new movements could not be accepted in America as easily as the earlier one. The French revolution of 1848, which inspired naturalism, had no equivalent in America. Courbet, the father of naturalism, was an ardent socialist, and the intellectual enthusiasm of the political doctrine conditioned his artistic attitude and that of his followers. Nothing of this kind could be said about the American painters of his period, for when the wave of naturalism eventually reached them, it had lost its ferocity. It could be said that the romantic realists in America ceased to be romantic because romanticism had died, and the realistic element remained.

Impressionism in France developed from naturalism and yet was a reaction against it at the same time. Courbet had painted the world as a picturesque experience. A warm tonality permeated the picture space, and the content was either a solemn sociological statement or stark reality. Manet, the founder of impressionism, increased the trend towards unification. His method consisted of splitting the form into particles of color and rearranging them so as to give the impression of reality seen through a veil of light and air. Courbet's tonality was cleared up until it changed into a mosaic of pure hues. Finally, the tenets of socialism were abandoned; all propaganda was excluded from the realm of painting. Art became an end in itself: *l'art pour l'art!*

Naturalism was not strong enough in America to engender an heir apparent—and also an opponent—as vigorous as impressionism. Yet, there were artists in America who groped their way towards the objectives achieved by the great masters in France. Their accomplishment is the more creditable because it was not carried by a mighty nation-wide stream, as was true on the Continent. It was an undercurrent only, but this undercurrent flowed in the same direction as the stream of creative evolution. The isolated experiments of these American painters prepared the way for a reception of modern art, again eliminating the time by which American lagged behind European developments.

On this side of the Atlantic, naturalism first appeared in the Currier and Ives lithographs found in every American home. Children grew up with them. The cheap prints were folk art in the same sense as the panorama was. Like the panorama the 'chromos' were not without influence on painters, although they belonged to a 'lower' level of artistic production frowned upon by cultivated people. Posterity is more interested in this 'lower' level of art than in the works of many of the skilled artists favored by society in their time. It is true that the Currier and Ives prints are uneven; but the best of them reach a rather high level, and their honest naïveté disarms the critic.

In 1863 Currier and Ives published a still life, a chromolithograph, which deserves special attention for its artistic quality (fig. 99). It is signed by Frances Palmer. This artist was born Frances Flora Bond in

Leicester, England, about 1812, to cultured but impoverished parents. The hope of better living conditions drove her and her husband, a Mr. Edward S. Palmer, to America. Thanks to an intensive artistic training enjoyed in Europe, she found employment as a draftsman with Currier and Ives. Her careful studies from nature went into many prints, but only a few of them carry her signature, because as a rule they were executed by several people. A frail but indefatigable woman, she worked until her death in 1876.

Her still life, a gorgeous array of flowers and fruits, is arranged in vases, bowls, and baskets on a table in an open porch. A lovely view of the Hudson River forms the background. Trumpet vines creeping up the trellis have attracted a hummingbird. Although the painter records all details carefully, and does not neglect the background, the painting creates a unified effect through a careful integration of all the forms included. There is no empty or confused spot in the picture. The lines intertwine elegantly and free themselves again without effort. This flawless composition is supported by a careful gradation of tones, and the color is equally bright and harmonious. No academic tradition weighed on the ill-bred child of the graphic arts, the chromo. This was only to the good of the offspring, for left to itself, the popular lithograph developed valuable qualities: truthfulness and luminosity. In other words, it partly anticipated naturalism and impressionism.

Not only in lithography, however, were the first steps taken towards naturalism and impressionism in the eighteen sixties. The portrait painter Edward Bowers, of whom we know very little, painted a remarkable still life in oil showing a decanter with red wine, an empty glass, grapes, pears, an apple, a knife, and a few broken biscuits on a bare table (fig. 101). The painting is dated 1865, at Detroit. Bowers, according to the city directory, lived there in 1866 and 1867. His painting, a small canvas, impresses us first through its bright and sonorous color. A second glance reveals the power with which textures are captured: the brush strokes are firm and unashamed of their original vigor. As a matter of fact, the transparent effect of the glass, and the spongy character of the cantaloupe are achieved by mere dexterity in the handling of the brush. The composition is strikingly unsymmetrical, but as with the Peales, the edge of the table is parallel to the lower edge of the picture. Although the style of the still life is fundamentally tonal and more picturesque than objectivist, its forms are clear-cut, and its general character is no less spare and sober than that of a Raphaelle Peale. The tradition of Philadelphia seems to have reappeared in the disguise of a naturalistic technique.

The still-life painter Andrew John Henry Way represents the same stage in the development of American still life as Bowers' still life with the decanter. Way was born in Washington, D. C., in 1826, studied in Europe and, after some attempts in other fields, specialized in still-life painting on the advice of Emanuel Leutze. The artist worked many years in Baltimore, but died in his native city in 1883. His contemporaries liked his work, and he was more successful than most of the 'little masters' of the American still life. The Peabody Institute of Baltimore owns an apple still life by Way that is painted with a certain sober charm (fig. 100). On the smooth top of a wooden table an overturned basket has emptied its contents of apples. The forms are clear and simple, while shadow and light are neatly distributed. The table is viewed from the side and thus appears somewhat slanting. As a whole the painting belongs decidedly to naturalistic art. It might be argued that it has a narrative overtone, for the painter seems to suggest that the grocer had placed rotten apples beneath the good ones; when the basket toppled over, the hidden shame came to the fore, a warning for shoppers; but the story is so slight that it does not change the naturalistic character of the picture.

Way was a good observer of the world around him. He evidently was interested in the appearance of everyday objects in bright daylight. His apple still life is no dull studio piece. It is, however, painted in a traditional technique. Of all varieties of the still life the close-up was most suitable to stimulate new methods in the representation of light and air. For this reason close-ups approximated impressionism at an astonishingly early time. The landscape painter Worthington Whittredge painted in 1867 a branch of an apple tree which is in no way behind its time. In fact, this painting, now in the Karolik Collection in Boston, could almost have been painted by a member of the French *avant-garde* of the time. This is surprising, for Whittredge had studied in Europe under the conservative Düsseldorf post-romanticist Andreas Achenbach, who continued the heritage of the Barbizon School. As a matter of fact, Whittredge in his long life (he died as late as 1910) only rarely attained again the freedom of expression shown in his early study, the *Branch of an Apple Tree*. Here he put the color on the canvas in rapid strokes, reacting quickly to the fleeting impressions that met his eyes. One feels the warmth of the sun on the smooth skin of the fruits. The background is reduced to a few blurred patches of color, a true representation of the actual impression the eye receives if it focuses on an object in the foreground. A charming water color *Laurel Blossoms in a Blue Vase* (fig. 103), undated but probably painted about ten years later, approaches the impressionism of the *Branch of an Apple Tree*.

Somewhat later than Whittredge painted his apples, an unknown American painter did a close-up of hollyhocks set against the fringe of a forest (fig. 104). It bears no date but seems to belong to the end of the 'seventies. The flower covers the greater part of the canvas, receiving full sunlight and contrasting effectively with the blue of the sky and the different shades of green in the landscape background. The handling of the color is less vigorous than that of Whittredge, but the method of representing grass and foliage by means of tiny dots contains the germ of an impressionistic technique.

Naturalism did not develop along a straight line into impressionism. Experiments were made that led into side paths. One of the most interesting painters of this experimental period in France was Monticelli. He broadened the brush strokes of Courbet into gushes of glowing color, achieving the effect of fireworks in contrast to the sunlight of the impressionists. In America Ralph Albert Blakelock (1847-1919) developed a similar style independently. With patches of color he tried to capture the effect of twilight or of moonlight. His technique approximates that in a mosaic, and makes it proper to list Blakelock among the naturalists and impressionists instead of the post-romanticists. He strove to poetize nature and seldom painted still lifes; when he did, flowers were his subject matter (fig. 102). His paintings are permeated by a melancholy that gradually turned into insanity—a strange coincidence, for Monticelli suffered the same fate. Extreme poverty might have contributed to Blakelock's breakdown, but was scarcely its cause.

The painters thus far discussed were not influenced by their French contemporaries. It was only natural, however, that American painters of French descent should go to study in Paris. For example, John La Farge, born in 1835 in New York to a French family of artistic culture, had his training in France. There, in the eighteen fifties, he associated himself with William Morris Hunt, the American apostle of Millet. It was through Hunt that La Farge was exposed to Millet's style, which was naturalistic with leanings towards idealism. La Farge later on told Royal Cortissoz:

In 1859 I aimed at making a realistic study of painting, keeping to myself the designs and attempts, serious or slight, which might have a meaning more than that of a strict copy from nature. I painted flowers to get the relation between the softness and the brittleness of the flower and the hardness of the bowl or whatever it might be in which the flower might be placed. Instead of arranging my subject, which is the usual studio way, I had it placed before me by chance, with any background and any light, leaving, for instance, the choice of flowers and vase to the servant girl or groom or any one else. Or else I copied the corner of the breakfast table as it happened to be.

La Farge's flower pieces of the 'sixties are closer to contemporary French art than anything in America at the time. As a matter of fact, they are broader than those of Fantin Latour, which they resemble at times; though only vaguely. The *Magnolia Grandiflora* in the Lawrence Art Museum (fig. 107) does not bear a date, but seems to have been dashed off while the influence of Paris was still fresh. Thus it must be dated about 1860. Its composition is highly unorthodox and its technique unusually bold. Another flower study, the *Calla Lily* in the collection of Professor Frank Jewett Mather, shows a similar but already more integrated style and is dated 1862 (fig. 106). The calla lily floats in the company of some other flowers in a tray of water. This arrangement is so strikingly informal that few artists in the 'sixties would have chosen it for a painting. The picture illustrates La Farge's statement to Cortissoz quoted above, for the flowers really appear in the picture as if they were arranged by chance. The casual quality of the motif, however, was not followed literally by the artist. He emphasized some parts and softened others. The white form of the lily stands out from the warm darkness of the background like a marble figure in the shadow of a dense grove. The aesthetic appeal of the picture is not achieved in a haphazard way. It is the result of careful organization.

Two years later La Farge visibly moved away from the naturalism of his earliest period: in his *Vase of Flowers* of 1864 nature is interpreted with an esoteric taste touching on mysticism (fig. 109). The flowers in a cylindrical vase look as if they had grown on the top of a broken column. Both the flowers and the receptacle almost melt into the indefinite brown background woven of strange plants. A slip of paper bearing the signature of the artist is on the table to the right of the vase, and a tiny flower lies on it. This delicate motif suggests a deeper meaning without revealing its significance. The vase itself is placed in the lower left corner of the picture space. This unusual arrangement creates a forlorn feeling, and the impression of the whole is enigmatic.

In 1865 La Farge again painted a close-up: *Holly-hocks and Corn*, set against an indistinct but luminous orange-yellow background (fig. 108). The green husks of the corn are torn open to show the yellow kernels. The painter, whose poetical and intellectual trend seems to have come more and more into the open,

dramatized the contrast between the blossoms, which reach out vigorously for the rays of the sun, and the fruit, which rests on the ground, heavy and open, ready to sink its seeds into the soil.

A year after this painting, literary propensities definitely gained ascendency over the pictorial value of La Farge's work. In 1866 he painted the *Wreath* (fig. 110), a work that openly acknowledges its symbolic inspiration, for it contains an explanatory inscription. A wreath is fastened on a bare stone wall, in such a way that the distances between the four edges of the picture and the circumference of the wreath are unequal. This arrangement produces an effect similar to that of the flower vase—an effect that I have interpreted as forlorn. Forlornness actually is the essence of the Greek inscription graven in the stone below the wreath: Θερεος Νεον Ισταμενοιο, 'As summer was just beginning,' an elegiac meditation evidently prompted by the death of a youthful person.

In spite of its symbolism, La Farge's *Wreath* is painted in the technique of naturalism. The time for a genuine pictorial symbolism had not arrived. The danger of eclecticism always threatens artists with symbolic leanings, and La Farge did not escape. In the 'seventies he abandoned his sound naturalism in favor of a more academic, decorative style. After about 1880 he devoted himself almost exclusively to the design of stained glass and to the creation of murals, which were executed mainly by his assistants. The promise of his beginnings as a pure painter was not fulfilled in his later work. He died in 1910 at Providence, Rhode Island, a famous man, but the lasting works he left were the unassuming paintings of his youth. In this respect, La Farge was not unique among his contemporaries. In Europe Adolf von Menzel is a striking example of a painter whose posthumous fame rests largely on the works of his youth and whose later paintings, more highly praised by his contemporaries, are dated. And it is not without significance that the beautiful works of Menzel's youth show for French naturalism an affinity that he gradually lost in later years.

The influence of Courbet reached America belatedly and indirectly, through Munich. The first of the many Americans who studied in Munich was Frank Duveneck; William Merrit Chase came next. Duveneck was born in 1848, Chase in 1849. Chase died in 1916. Duveneck survived him by three years. It was their generation that introduced the methods of the Munich studios in America: methods stressing the portrayal of textures, a warm and rich tonality, and an *alla prima* technique that delighted in the display of elegant brush strokes. Both had distinguished careers as teachers, apart from their successes as artists. Duveneck painted still lifes only occasionally; they are dashing exercises of the brush (fig. 105). Chase made still-life painting an integral part of his *œuvre*. An eclectic by temperament, he developed a standard type of composition modeled after the Dutch kitchen pieces. The silvery skin of fishes is cleverly contrasted with the shiny surface of brass or copper pans (figs. 111 and 112).

Emil Carlsen, slightly younger, succeeded Chase as the favorite American still-life painter at the end of the nineteenth century. Born in Copenhagen, Denmark, in 1853 and trained there as an architectural draftsman, he developed into an artist only after he had come to America as a young man. A sojourn in Paris left its mark on his painting although he was engaged there in commercial art production. His still lifes are not strong, but at their best have a distinct feminine charm (figs. 113 and 114). Carlsen died in 1932.

The Boston-born painter Abbott Henderson Thayer (1849-1921) was in Paris in 1875, ten years ahead of Carlsen. The idealizing tendency that made his ambitious figure compositions successful during his lifetime has proved to be an obstacle to their appreciation a generation later. In painting dead fowl he was in his true element, for he was an amateur zoologist. His honest and tasteful way of painting finds its happiest expression in his still lifes (fig. 116). The result comes close to that of Courbet and Schuch (fig. 13) thanks to an impeccable technique and a natural gift for portraying textures. An otherwise unknown American painter L. Koechlin created a similar still life with fowl in 1890 (fig. 117).

Among the Americans who discovered the impressionists in Paris for themselves at an early date, J. Alden Weir (1852-1919) alone painted still lifes more than occasionally. Only in the earliest of them did he keep himself free from the general decay of form characterizing so many of the foreign followers of the great French pioneers. For his *Delft Plate* (1888) Weir was evidently inspired by Manet (fig. 115). The way in which the peaches are built up with nervous strokes of the brush, that in which the pewter of the beer mug is dissolved in patches of color conveying the impression of lights—this is early impressionism at its best. The composition displays a trend towards asymmetry and towards the inclusion of empty areas, which came to the French impressionists from Japan.

Of Childe Hassam (1859-1935), who translated Claude Monet into the American idiom, only a few fruit and flower pieces are known. By their abbreviated style, they sometimes suggest Chinese wash drawings (fig. 119).

Frederick Carl Friesecke (1874-1939) did not so much Americanize as popularize French impressionism. In his attractive garden and boudoir scenes, he adapted its formulas to the traditional taste. When he chose a bunch of wild flowers for a model instead of a girl in a tempting negligee, he escaped the danger of being commonplace to which he often succumbed and displayed a well-trained and not too heavy hand (fig. 118).

William J. Glackens of Philadelphia (1870-1938) was, next to Twachtmann, the most important among the American impressionists. He was a press illustrator by profession, and in this capacity acquired a humble devotion to reality from which his painting benefited. His style was patterned after Renoir, but he was too much of an American and too much of a reporter to follow Renoir into his most personal realm. For this realm was exclusively French. Renoir never was a realist. His lyric interpretation of nature was difficult to reconcile to the training of a draftsman like Glackens, whose strength was the ability to grasp the hard facts of daily life in the big cities. Glackens never followed Renoir in dissolving form into a web of color fibers. He only enriched the appearance of his paintings by imitating Renoir's technique and color. Nor did he follow the French impressionists in their avoidance of symmetry in their compositions. Glackens liked well-balanced arrangements, and built his compositions with more traditional taste. Wherever it was possible, he made his flowers form regular patterns (fig. 120).

Unlike Glackens, who struggled against firmly rooted realism in his quest for an impressionistic style, Arthur Clifton Goodwin (Boston, 1863-1929) intuitively found his way towards impressionism without being encumbered with a realistic tradition. He was self-taught. Like Gauguin, he was a business man before he began to paint. And he never became famous as a member of a group of American impressionists. However, this had an advantage, for Goodwin's isolated position among the painters at the turn of our century prevented him from becoming doctrinal. His street scenes and landscapes aroused the vivid interest of the noted Italian art historian Lionello Venturi, who considers Goodwin one of the best, if not the most genuine, American impressionist. In fact, his painting is amazingly fresh and free.

Goodwin's still lifes are few. They are quick notes jotted down with pastels in an inspired moment, not well-constructed compositions. The painter had a remarkably light touch (fig. 121). He used the medium of the pastel as a clever conversationalist uses language. Witty, improvising his effects, he captured the spirit of a moment. He had grace, elegance, and culture, and his elective affinity for French art was genuine.

Arthur Clifton Goodwin came as close to the serene quality of French impressionism as a foreigner can without living in Paris permanently and being fully acclimated. There remained an inevitable gap, for America has neither the Gallic spirit nor the silvery air of the Ile de France that generated French impressionism. The strength of American painting lay in another field. American impressionism was a stage in the development of an international standard rather than a goal in itself. For that reason impressionistic still-life painting was no more than a pleasant but short interlude in the history of American art.

VII. THE GROWTH OF PRECISIONISM

IN THE last quarter of the nineteenth century Paris gradually supplanted Munich as an attraction for American art students, but it was not before 1900 that the work of Cézanne and Van Gogh began to impress itself on some of the newcomers. At that time was formed the fluctuating and cosmopolitan group of post-impressionists known today as the School of Paris.

One of the earliest Americans who came into the orbit of this new group was Maurice Prendergast. Born in Boston in 1859, he went to Paris first in 1884 and stayed there for five years; but only during his second visit to the French capital in 1897-8 did he discover Cézanne. Deeply impressed, he immediately tried out what he had learned from his study of Cézanne by painting a series of water colors on Venetian themes. Back in America, he developed an all but two-dimensional style that combined the decorative pattern of Gauguin with the dynamic line of Van Gogh. About the same time the Norwegian Edward Munch developed a similar style independently. He too received his inspiration from the French post-impressionists in Paris.

Not until he was in his late fifties, when illness made it difficult for him to paint out of doors, did Prendergast begin painting still lifes. First his subjects were flowers, which offered him the opportunity of building up compositions of pure color (fig. 122); later on his motifs were arrangements of fruit, bottles and jars—the same type of objects that served Cézanne to demonstrate his principles of color architecture. The American disciple of the French master enlarged Cézanne's small 'color bricks' into heavy 'color stones.' In France at an earlier date Signac had developed Seurat's round color dots into massive, almost rectangular patches. Prendergast handled these elements in a way similar to that of the French pointillists. His development had not come to a standstill when he died in 1924.

Adolphe Borie, a Philadelphian (1877-1934), became engrossed in the subtler aspect of Cézanne and learned from the master how to express form with color by means of a methodical arrangement of tones. A still life of *Stone Fruit* exemplifies this device (fig. 123). Later on, Borie tended to subordinate form to color—a development that parallels that of the *Fauves*, a group of French painters who collected around Matisse.

Max Weber, also a resident of Paris during his formative years, was influenced by Cézanne and the Douanier Rousseau. From their examples he developed a half-refined, half-primitive style. Maurice Stern, influenced by the early experiments of the cubists, painted still lifes in angular forms, and Alexander Brook channeled the esoteric spirit of the School of Paris into a pictorial language that was easily understandable, intelligent, and attractive. All these artists, and many of their younger colleagues, including the sensitive Julian Levi and the refined Yasuo Kuniyoshi, produced competent still lifes without overstepping the intellectual radius of the School of Paris, even after they had settled in New York and had become integral elements of the art life of America. Their influence on the public taste has been most wholesome: it balanced the nationalistic tendencies that threatened to establish a new brand of the old provincialism under the slogan of Americanism.

There is, however, a genuine American tradition in colonial times which has been demonstrated by Oscar Hagen, and which, as has been shown earlier in this book, can be traced through the nineteenth century. It is a tradition of seeing that may be called matter of fact, detached, sober, spare, puritan—terms that in different degrees characterize the still-life paintings of the Peales, Francis, and Harnett, not to speak of the work of numerous isolated and unknown primitive painters. Like all true traditions, it cannot be molded into a popular program and it is far from being a strict doctrine valid for the whole nation or for an indefinite time. It is much too subtle a thing to be gained through the mere illustration of the 'American scene' and its negative concomitant, the rejection of the aesthetic heritage of Europe. For the development of art is a continuous process: what may seem revolutionary at the first glance, may actually be the reappearance of a hitherto latent undercurrent. An obscure undercurrent becomes manifest at a moment of history when the spirit of the time runs parallel to the trend of the dormant tradition. In its new manifest state the former undercurrent, whose development has all but ceased, follows the cyclic changes of the period styles.

Each era produces a dominant feature that influences all aspects of life in its sphere. Take the Baroque, for example: its most pregnant creation was the modern theater, which strove to create the illusion of reality. Consequently the imprint of the theater appeared in all aspects of the civilization of the Baroque period: politics and architecture, religion and painting. Just as dissolved matter, invisible in water, at a given impulse solidifies in the significant form of crystals around a kernel, so the isolated elements of social life gather around a cultural nucleus and assume a unified structural character. The process of cultural crystallization begins with faint symptoms and only gradually reveals its tendency. Today, such a process of crystallization has become evident: it is the change of society under the influence of mechanization.

Mechanization became a crystallizing force in modern American art no less than the theater did in Baroque art. A modern American painter cannot help being influenced by mechanization, for mass production on the assembly line, to cite the most impressive application of mechanization, came to be of the greatest consequence for all manifestations of American life.

The influence of industrial design on modern art is obvious to the most superficial observer. Early in the present century, the American architect Frank Lloyd Wright, more than anybody else, promoted the reconciliation of art and industry, but the aesthetic consequence of the new development was grasped abroad more keenly than in this country. The *Bauhaus* in Germany methodically applied the teachings of mechanization to all forms of art.

Mechanization is the product of a distinctly American way of thinking. In the last analysis the thought process that led to the phenomenon of mechanization began with the founding of the United States; that is, with the adoption of the French Enlightenment as the philosophical basis of the new republic. When Jefferson designed a convertible chair with an adjustable reading desk, this contraption anticipated the patent furniture of the nineteenth century. The technological way of thinking was in competition with Jefferson's artistic credo, classicism.

In his book *L'Homme machine*, the French philosopher of the Enlightment period Lamettrie had spread the concept—much discussed during the late eighteenth century—that man is an engine. The early enthusiasm for things mechanical that in Lamettrie's philosophy found a less profound than startling expression, influenced the arts as well as other activities. In using the camera obscura and the pantograph, the painter was not considered to be weakening his technique but rather strengthening it. The flawlessly precise architectural views of the two Canalettos offer striking examples of the influence of the early period of mechanization on painting. And we know that Charles Willson Peale used the pantograph.

The same reliance on mechanization subsequently permeated the whole of America and stimulated similar developments. From objectivism and the panoramic landscape to the *trompe l'œil* style, the trend towards mechanical exactness increased rather than diminished, and it was to be expected that photography would follow the peep show, the camera obscura, the pantograph, and the panorama as a stimulating influence in American painting.

Precision, which again and again appeared as a characteristic of American still-life painting, eventually became the main objective of a movement that developed after the First World War and was immediately dubbed 'precisionism' by alert critics.

This trend evolved from the experiments of three painters who worked independently: Charles Demuth, Preston Dickinson, and Charles Sheeler. They never developed a school, even of the loosely knit form of the French impressionists. There was practically no exchange of ideas among the three men, two of whom, Dickinson and Demuth, died prematurely, except that Charles Daniel, a New York art dealer, repeatedly showed their works together in his gallery and thus underlined their common traits.

The common denominator of the group was, as indicated by the term itself, a marked tendency towards precision, a tendency not restricted to America, however. In Germany a group of painters advocated precision under the slogan 'Neue Sachlichkeit,' but in contrast to the American precisionists, they subordinated this principle to metaphysical interpretation of the visual world. The Europeans lacked the psychological background that made the Americans, accepting mechanization as a normal way of life, feel at home in a world of ruler-drawn highways and crystalline skyscrapers.

Charles Demuth was the first American painter who undertook to adapt the achievements of French post-impressionism to the American feeling for mechanization. Born in Lancaster, Pennsylvania, in 1882, he was trained first at the Pennsylvania Academy of Fine Arts, but it was only in Paris, where he sojourned several times between 1911 and 1913, that he found himself. From 1921 to his premature death in 1935 he divided his time between his home, Cape Cod, and the coast of Maine. Both the rigid smokestacks of Pennsylvania steel mills and the clear-cut gables of old New England houses inspired him to an abstract interpretation of forms in which he reduced French cubism to a planimetric system of lines. This was the nature of his work immediately after the First World War. At about the same time he began to be interested in still-life painting, especially in flowers and fruits (figs. 124, 125, 126). With loving eyes he followed the flowing lines of the stems of daisies and the curves of fruits, took in the elegant lancet forms of leaves and the fluffy petals of spring blossoms. Being primarily a water-color artist, he soon overcame the mathematical formula of his architectural studies and developed a sensitive style. He often left the background of his still lifes white, and these recall the work of primitive painters from the beginning of the nineteenth century (fig. 40). It was the art form of the close-up, however, in which he expressed himself most happily. The delicate tangle of weeds, the silver bells of a set of calla lilies, the pattern of fruits and foliage in a plum tree—these were the motifs that gave him the best chance of developing his innate love of precision, not the world of steel construction. Very transparent, subdued, and pure colors add to the dainty and fastidious effect of his art. Demuth's precisionism was a subtle guiding force rather than a principle. It led him to results which, at least in his close-ups of plants, recall Dürer's minute studies of similar motifs. To sum up, he was, like Stephen Vincent Benét, at home on both sides of the Atlantic without being an expatriate.

Preston Dickinson was eight years younger than Demuth; he was born in New York in 1891 and died in Spain in 1930. A pupil of the Art Student's League in New York, he came into contact with the impressionist tradition through Ernest Lawson and acquired a taste for the decorative quality of Japanese color prints. Fitted out with these not at all unusual prerequisites, he went to Paris. It was a propitious moment for his introduction to Paris art circles. His mind was no less searching than Demuth's, and Cézanne's doctrine had just begun to emerge from pointillism and other competing theories as the supreme challenge to the young generation of artists. Whereas Demuth had the reserve of a somewhat more advanced personality and calmly accepted the new principles, Dickinson was young enough to be swept off his feet completely. For five years, from 1910 to 1915, he painted little, engrossed in the all-absorbing task of assimilating Cézanne. Prendergast had understood Cézanne only vaguely, but Dickinson did not cease before he had penetrated the inner sanctum. He grasped the idea of interpreting space through color, that is, of substituting an infinitely subtle system of color planes for the traditional compromise between form and color. Being a man of keen acumen, he did not aspire to the master's own crown. He knew his own possibilities and limitations, which had been determined by his American background. The transparent and enchanted style of Cézanne had grown from the style of sublime colorists, the French School. The gentle veil covering the Ile de France and the mild harmony of the Mediterranean Coast are not to be found in America; and in the figurative sense the mild climate of French culture softens the harshness of modern life. America's intellectual atmosphere, on the other hand, is too hard and too matter of fact to engender an art closely akin to that of the French.

Dickinson attacked his problem by first substituting products of a machine civilization for the products of handicraft that served Cézanne as models for his still lifes. Still life, he had no doubt, was the *via regia* to the new painting. His wine bottles, cocktail mixers, steel knives, and cooking pans served him to develop a style hard enough to express his innate way of seeing things, and at the same time they gave him the means of simplifying Cézanne's formula until it approximated the aesthetics of the rule-drawn highways and the crystalline skyscrapers (figs. 128, 129). Now, America is not only harder than Europe, it is also more dynamic. Accordingly, Dickinson looked for a master who could complement the static style of Cézanne with dynamics, but would still be fundamentally compatible with Cézanne. Such a master he found in El Greco, and thus moved to Spain eventually. The dynamism of El Greco, however, springs from a source different from that of America—it is a religious dynamism; whereas the American dynamism is of the powerhouse. Nevertheless Dickinson managed to draw a most valuable inspiration from El Greco, a kind of spiritual quality of which the external sign is the elongation of forms that characterized Dickinson's late works. This spiritual element also influenced his choice of themes. Flowers enter his severe world, and although he did not interpret them with the refined touch of Demuth, he grasped their essence most convincingly, as illustrated in a magnificent vase with tulips, which shows him at the peak of his short career (fig. 127). Here he has arranged all forms into a perfect pattern of volumes without freezing the life out of the flowers and without distorting the objects into absurd mathematical shapes. The simple and convincing color scale matches the lucidity of his space concept. Dickinson's precisionism was on the threshold of becoming a valid American style of painting when his early death occurred.

Fortunately the last of the three painters who moved towards similar goals, Charles Sheeler, has been allowed to reach a full maturity and is among us, vigorous and creative, attaining a higher degree of perfection with every new work. He was born in 1883 in Philadelphia. Like Demuth he entered the Art Academy of his home city, and like Demuth too he was dissatisfied with his training, although they did not attend the same classes. He studied what nowadays we should call design, and Demuth studied what occasionally is still called fine arts. But eventually Sheeler too joined the adepts of the nobler branch, and that under its educational high priest, William M. Chase. Chase preached what in Parisian studios later on was labeled *Munichoiserie*, by a witty modification of the word *Chinoiserie*. The elegant technique of Chase could not hold the young draftsman's imagination for any length of time, especially after a studio trip to Europe with his teacher introduced Sheeler to the Old Masters whom Chase imitated superficially. Further travel in Italy, undertaken with a congenial friend in 1909, opened Sheeler's eyes to the values of form, and a subsequent stay in Paris brought him in touch with the *avant-garde* that was about to develop cubism and fauvism. The intellectual curiosity of the young American drew him to the new phenomena, and his deep-rooted honesty made him analyze what he saw in the spirit of fairness.

After his return to America he decided to make his living as an industrial photographer rather than to try the impossible: to sell post-impressionist paintings in an America still not quite sure about the soundness of impressionism. The choice of industrial photography certainly was not a matter of chance. It was a satisfactory way for him, since practicing visual honesty was an asset in this profession. It was congenial work, for the lens is the most precise draftsman, and precision was natural and essential to Sheeler as an artist. Not without very good reason, Constance Rourke, the brilliant biographer of Sheeler, termed him 'an artist in the American tradition'; for it was the genuine American attitude towards the visual world—exact, scientific, and calmly detached—that animated Sheeler's work from the beginning. Whereas in Europe the in-

vention of photography wrought havoc among the established values of art, it proved to be a constructive element in American art, at least in the hands of the right man. Sheeler was the right man. The possibilities of a true photographic style were conceived at about the same time by him, Edward Steichen, and Paul Strand. For a long time previously, photography had tried to compete with etching and charcoal drawing, only to produce hybrid effects. Alfred Stieglitz had paved the way for a revolution in photography. Now, in the hands of competent men, photography matured.

Sheeler lived at the time in an eighteenth-century Pennsylvania house of clear-cut design. Studying his surroundings, he developed a strictly objectivist style in photography, preferring the simple frontal view and the juxtaposition of carefully selected textures to interesting angles and picturesque effects. Engineering architecture and the functional interiors of the Shakers, that sect of practical mystics in Pennsylvania, attracted him by their rigid forms. Using the teachings of photography to sharpen his sense of form, he developed a new style as a painter. This style, however, is photographic only in so far as its precision is inspired and consciously trained by the study of photography. Sheeler's style is equally indebted to cubism, for its fundamental quality is the clarity with which he grasps the relation of the volumes to each other. Sheeler stated personally that visual interpretation of the space between the objects is his main objective. As a result, Sheeler has attained a highly abstract style in spite of his eminent capacity to record the 'detailed appearances of a new world,' to quote a neat formula by John Everett Austin, Jr. Sheeler's method of digesting reality is a slow process—a pertinent reason why still life is his main province. Like Harnett, but for different reasons, he has eliminated the human figure almost altogether from his world; and his eye, keen and objective, grasps the pregnant view of every *Gestalt*. Whether it is a corner of a room with characteristically spare and smooth furniture or a table covered with severely shaped glass and chaste white china, whether discarded tires or cactus plants are his models, the precision of an unerring perception penetrates their appearance and from insignificant objects distills the elements of a new beauty (figs. 130, 131, 133). This beauty is far from being cold, for Sheeler is as gentle and sensitive as any refined painter ever was. He paints a spring bouquet, and despite the detached and almost puritan character of the composition, the picture is full of an enchanting music of the heart (fig. 132). On the other hand, when he records the form of the wheels, of the transmission, and of the cylinder of a modern locomotive, he seems to fulfil the promise of the unknown painter of the *Locomotive at Night*, who half a century earlier groped his way with scant artistic means to a new interpretation of machinery (fig. 134). Sheeler's interpretation of the machine, in all its apparent austerity, is eminently human, for it lovingly and lucidly displays the intricate mechanical design as a work of the mind. In Sheeler's work mechanization is being humanized. Hence he not only forms the zenith of a development but also points the way to a new goal.

VIII. SUMMING UP

STILL-LIFE painting originated in Europe during the Renaissance, and since then several types of still lifes have been developed. The painter was interested either in the objects themselves, in a detached, objective way, or in the picturesque effect of objects, as they appear under various atmospheric conditions and light effects. He finally could intensify reality to such a degree as to trick the eye into accepting the painting as reality. The first type of still-life painting is called in this discussion 'objectivist,' and its style is linear. The style of the second, the picturesque still life, a product of the Baroque, is tonal. The third type, illusionist, which was stimulated by a new interest in optics, is known as the *trompe l'œil*. Its heightened realism creates an uncanny effect.

The first step towards still-life painting in America was the decorative flower painting of the Pennsylvania Germans. It was developed during the eighteenth century as design for painted furniture and other objects. The folk art of the Pennsylvania Germans flourished until the middle of the nineteenth century. Folk art creates an atmosphere favorable for higher art forms. This became evident in Philadelphia, which about 1810 became the birthplace of American still-life painting as an independent art form.

The first still lifes of the Philadelphia School were fruit and flower pieces painted in an accurate, detailed, and glossy style, which had been developed for use in illustrating impressive botanical works published in France at the end of the eighteenth century. The illustrators of these works adapted the Dutch tradition of fruit and flower painting to the needs of natural history. The chiaroscuro of the Baroque was supplanted by the clarity of classicism, and the objective representation of fruit and flowers was heightened into an aesthetic experience. I have suggested the term 'botanic-decorative' for this school of still-life painters. Botanic-decorative still-life painting was a by-product of the rationalist movement in philosophy known in France as the Enlightenment. From the time of the Declaration of Independence, this philosophy has been an important element of American thought. Its concomitant in painting was a trend towards exactness of reproduction. This trend came to the fore in the panoramic landscape of the Hudson River School and in the revival of the *trompe l'œil* during the nineteenth century. The first was preceded by the panorama, the second by the peep show. The panoramic landscape expressed the space feeling of America in the years of the Western expansion by means of a new variety of illusionism. The revival of *trompe l'œil* painting was stimulated by the materialistic taste of the 'gilded decades,' but sensitive artists were able to overcome the limitations of materialistic aesthetics. They developed the *trompe l'œil* into a superrealistic style in which still-life objects were interpreted symbolically.

The same intellectual trend that in the nineteenth century produced the panoramic landscape and the style of *trompe l'œil* produced the artistic movement of precisionism in the twentieth century. Precisionism was inspired by photography, and it served to capture and at the same time to humanize the mechanistic traits of modern American civilization.

Another American phenomenon is the survival of primitive art during the nineteenth century. American primitives—still-life painters and others alike—gave expression to the creative energies formerly channeled into the crafts. In the middle of the nineteenth century, America also contributed exquisite *genre* and still-life painters to the art of romantic realism that flourished on both sides of the Atlantic.

Naturalism and impressionism were imported from Europe comparatively late, but were anticipated by creditable works of isolated American artists. In all phases of the history of American still-life painting,

Philadelphia retained a leading role. This, however, does not mean that American still-life painting was lacking in universality.

Seen as a whole, the development of American still-life painting shows an amazing continuity wherein lies its importance, for continuity is the essence of culture. The quiet labor of American still-life painters has, after all, achieved what more ambitious movements failed to materialize: the establishment of a consistent American tradition.

NOTES

Source material not included in the annotation has been taken from the following dictionaries and reference books:

Samuel Greene Wheeler Benjamin, *Art in America*, New York, 1880.

Clara Erskine Clement (Waters) and Laurens Hutton, *Artists of the Nineteenth Century*, Boston, 1907.

Mantle Fielding, *Dictionary of American Painters, Sculptors and Engravers*, Philadelphia, 1925.

Mary E. Frankenhauser, *Biographical Sketches of American Artists*, Michigan State Library, Lansing, 1924.

Samuel Isham, *The History of American Painting . . . new ed.,*

with supplemental chapters by Royal Cortissoz, New York, 1927.

Evelyn Rila Jackman, *American Arts*, Chicago, 1928.

Ralph Clifton Smith, A *Biographical Index of American Artists*, Baltimore, 1930.

Ulrich Thieme and Felix Becker, *Allgemeines Lexikon der bildenden Künstler von der Antike bis zur Gegenwart*, Leipzig, 1907-.

In the following notes, the first figure indicates the page to which the reference is made, the second figure, the line; a indicates the left-hand column, b the right-hand column.

STATING THE PROBLEM

3:18a Wolfgang Born, 'Notes on Still-Life Painting,' *Antiques*, L, September 1946, pp. 158-60.

I: SOURCES AND PARALLELS

5:4a Max J. Friedländer, *On Art and Connoisseurship*, 2nd ed., London, 1943, p. 132, fig. 17.

5:30a Karl Voll, *Hans Memling*, Stuttgart, 1909, lists the painting as attributed to the master, but does not consider the attribution certain. In the context of this discussion it is of no great importance whether the painting is by the master himself or by one of his followers. It evidently is inspired by Memling.

5:7b Gustav Glück, *Die Kunst der Renaissance in Deutschland, den Niederlanden, Frankreich . . .* , 2nd ed., Berlin, 1928, p. 22, fig. 144.

5:20b D. Coke, *Confessions of an Incurable Collector*, London, 1928, ch. VI, pp. 54-63. Wolfgang Born, 'Early Peep-Shows and the Renaissance Stage,' *The Connoisseur*, CXII, 1941, pp. 67-71, 161, 180. Edgar Preston Richardson, 'Samuel van Hoogstraten and Carel Fabritius,' *Art in America*, XXV, 1937, pp. 141-52. R. H. Wilenski, *An Introduction to Dutch Art*, London, 2nd impression, reprinted 1937, p. 266: 'Houbraken bears witness to Hoogstraten's passionate interest in optics, and he relates that his house was full of cardboard representations of fruit, fish and so forth which appeared to have three dimensions.'

5:25b Robert Gavelle, 'La Réalité et son imitation suggérée: aspects de trompe l'œil,' *L'Amour de l'art*, XIX, Paris,

1938, p. 231. 'Trompe l'œil,' *The Illustrated London News* (Christmas Number), London, 1938, pp. 11-16. Elizabeth du Gue Trapier, 'Correa and trompe l'œil,' *Notes Hispanic*, 1945, pp. 15-30.

6:32a Herbert Furst, *The Art of Still-Life Painting*, London, 1927. Arthur Edwin Bye, *Pots and Pans*, Princeton, N. J., 1921. Arthur Everett Austin, Jr., *The Painters of Still Life, An Exhibition of the Wadsworth Atheneum*, Hartford, Conn., 1938.

6:39a G. I. Hoogewerff, ' "Nature Morte" Italiane del Seicento e del Settecento,' in *Dedalo*, IV, 1923-4: part I, pp. 599-624; part II, pp. 710-30.

6:46a Ralph Warner, *Dutch and Flemish Flower and Fruit Painters of the* XVIIth *and* XVIIIth *Centuries*, London, c. 1928. E. Zarnowska, *La Nature Morte Hollandaise*, Brussels, 1929. Julio Cavestany, *Sociedad Española de Amigos del Arte, Floreros y Bodegones*, Madrid, 1936-40.

6:9b Austin, op. cit. no. 19 (illustrated).

6:25b Ibid. no. 16 (illustrated).

6:50b Especially Juan Valdes Leal. Compare: Werner Weisbach, *Die Kunst des Barock*, Berlin, 1924, p. 114 and fig. 548.

7:8a Julius von Schlosser, *Kunst und Wunderkammern der Spätrenaissance*, Leipzig, 1908.

7:26a Wolfgang Born, 'Fetish, Amulet and Talisman,' *Ciba Symposia*, VII, 1945, pp. 102-32.

7:2b Op. cit. *The Illustrated London News* includes a reproduction of Haintz's painting.

7:19b Furst, op. cit. p. 215.

7:30b Gavelle, op. cit. (illustrated), p. 234.

7:39b Germain Bazin, 'L. B. Oudry, Animalier, dessinateur et paysagiste,' *L'Art et les artistes*, nouvelle série, XVII, 1929, pp. 109-115.

7:41b Furst, op. cit. p. 223.

7:45b G. Harrisse, *Boilly*, Paris, 1898, no. 580, p. 138.

7:50b N. S. Trivas, 'Les Natures mortes de Liotard,' *Gazette des Beaux-Arts*, 6th series, XV, 1936, pp. 307-10.

8:13a Warner, op. cit. Pl. 11, d.

8:15a Ibid. pl. 17, d.

8:26a Ibid. pl. 48, a.

8:38a E. P. Richardson, 'The Romantic Prelude to Dutch Realism,' *The Art Quarterly*, III, 1940, p. 54, fig. 5. Warner, op. cit. pl. 66, a.

8:15b 'Gerardus van Spaendonck,' *La Renaissance de l'art*, IX, 1932, p. 9. Jan Frans van Dael (b. Antwerp, 1746, d. Paris, 1840) painted flower pieces in a style similar to that of Spaendonck.

8:39b T. W. Earp, *Flower Still-Life Painting*, London, 1928, p. 12, correctly states: 'The growing interest in science, exhilarated by such a naturalist as Buffon or botanist as Rousseau, had caused in France the production of a great many beautifully engraved books, dealing with nature from the scientific rather than the artistic point of view. It is in the pages of the early botanies and natural histories, with their beautifully coloured plates of flowers, birds, or insects, that we find the final French culmination of Van Huysum and De Heem.' In the next paragraph, however, the author fails to trace the influence of botanic illustration on flower painting. He continues as follows: 'The form became a branch of literature rather than of art. From the stately volumes issued by the Royal Library before and after the Revolution, to the delicate vanities of the ladies' "Keepsakes" there still glow the beauty of the petal, the lustre of the butterfly's wing. But from the serious canvas such delicate objects have been banned.' For a still life by Lance, 'Fruit,' see ibid. pl. 21.

8:46b Helmuth P. Seckel, 'Francisco de Zurbarán as a Painter of Still Life,' MS. Martin S. Soria, 'Zurbarán, Right or Wrong,' *Art in America*, XXXII, 1944, pp. 126-41; 'Francisco de Zurbarán, a Study of his Style,' *Gazette des Beaux-Arts*, 6th series, XXV, 1944, pp. 33-40, 153-74.

9:18a No biographical data about Perez de Aguilar are available. His style shows the influence of the noted Mexican painter Miguel Cabrera (1695-1768). See: The Museum of Modern Art, *Twenty Centuries of Mexican Art* (catalogue), New York, 1940, pp. 90. 183.

9:33a Tarnowska, op. cit. XXV.

9:43a Earp, op. cit. p. 16.

9:44b Franz Roh, *Nach-Expressionismus. Magischer Realismus, Probleme der neuesten europäischen Malerei*, Leipzig, 1925.

II: IN QUEST OF THE OBJECT

10:4b Howard Mumford Jones, *America and French Culture*, 1750-1848, Chapel Hill, The University of North Carolina Press, 1927, pp. 365-87, 400-411.

10:7b John Walker and Macgill James, *Great American Paintings from Smibert to Bellows*, 1729-1928, New York, 1933, pl. 16. Metropolitan Museum of Art, *Life in America* (catalogue), New York, 1939, p. 40.

10:13b Charles Coleman Sellers, *The Artist of the Revolution. The Early Life of Charles Willson Peale*, Hebron, Connecticut, 1939. James Thomas Flexner, *America's Old Masters*, New York, 1939, pp. 171-244.

11:4a *Bulletin of the Museum of Fine Arts*, Boston, XXXIX, 1941, p. 42, fig. on p. 44.

11:16a John I. H. Baur, 'The Peales and the Development of American Still Life,' *The Art Quarterly*, III, 1940, pp. 283-4.

11:14b Ibid. pp. 88-91.

12:14a Ibid. pp. 81-3. An anonymous painting shows Raphaelle Peale holding the brush awkwardly in his gouty hand. In the background an apple still life on the wall. Compare: 'The Gifted Peale Family Added Glory to U. S. Art,' *Life Magazine*, XII, 1942, no. 13, p. 64.

12:43b Photograph in the Frick Art Reference Library, New York City, N. Y.

12:45b *Star Presentation, Pennsylvania Academy of the Fine Arts* (Exhibition catalogue), 1945, nos. 24, 25.

14:31b Baur, op. cit. fig. 4. The attribution to James Peale was based on information obtained from an art dealer who owned the picture. No document supported the statement.

15:28a In 1821-2 Rubens Peale was manager of another museum that his brother Rembrandt founded in Baltimore. I owe the information about Rubens Peale to Mr. Charles Coleman Sellers of Wesleyan University, Middletown, Conn.

15:52a E. P. Richardson, 'On Wings of Art,' *Art News*, XLIV, 1945, no. 14, p. 22. Clyde H. Burroughs, 'Paintings by the Peales,' *Bulletin of the Detroit Institute of Arts of the City of Detroit*, XXIII, 1944, no. 6, p. 58. Mr. Charles Coleman Sellers, in a letter addressed to me on 14 Jan. 1946, wrote about the 'Grouse in the Underbrush': 'as I understand they were painted from mounted specimens. Recently Edmund Bury (Philadelphia) had a number of stuffed grouse and was able to set them up so that they reproduced a picture.' Mr. Bury in a letter of 25 Jan. 1946 informed Mr. Sellers that the picture in question was by Titian Peale. It showed a male and a female quail. The stuffed specimen came from the home of Rubens Peale and probably belonged to his museum. It was suggested to Mr. Bury that they might have been taxidermized by a Mr. Bell, who lived part of the time with the Rubens Peale family and was thought to be related to them in some way. The picture and the two stuffed quail are now in a private collection in Bryn Mawr, Pa.

15:32b Wolfgang Born, 'The Female Peales: Their Art and Its Tradition,' *American Collector*, XV, Aug. 1946, pp. 12-14.

16:12a *Bulletin of the Municipal Museum of Baltimore*, II, 1942. M. Breuning, 'Peale Family Exhibitions, Walker Gallery,' *Magazine of Art*, XXXII, 1939, pp. 181-2.

16:16a Theodore Bolton, *Early American Portrait Painters in Miniature*, New York, 1921, p. 128.

16:9b *Bulletin of the Metropolitan Museum of Art*, XXXVII, 1942, pp. 43-4.

16:25b Henry Pleasants, Jr., *Four Great Artists of Chester County*, 1935, pp. 51-60, 'George Cope—The Realist.'

III: PRIMITIVES AND AMATEURS

17:17b Wolfgang Born, 'American Primitives, Europe, and the Orient,' *Antiques* (in press).

17:35b Jean Lipman, *American Primitive Painting*, New York, 1942, fig. 7.

18:12a E. Willard Emerson Keyes, 'Leading a Respectable Life,' *Antiques*, VIII, 1925, no. 90, fig. 1.

18:52a Esther Stevens Fraser, 'Pennsylvania Bride Boxes and Dower Chests,' *Antiques*, VII, 1925. For county types of chests, pp. 80-84, cf. fig. 2, 'Lebanon County Chest,' dated 1721, oldest known example decorated with flowers in a pot. Fig. 7, 'Dauplin County Chest,' dated 1805. decorated with flower vases and birds.

18:29b *American Folk Art* (catalogue), Williamsburg, Virginia, 1940, pp. 33, 34, no. 140.

18:36b Op. cit. Montenegro, fig. 59.

19:37a *The Old Print Shop Portfolio*, I, 1941, no. 24.

20:23a Harry B. Wehle and Theodore Bolton, *American Miniatures*, 1730-1856, New York, 1927, pl. 39.

20:42a Baur, op. cit. p. 91.

20:16b Furst, op. cit. p. 213.

IV: ROMANTIC INFLUENCES

21:16a C. E. Sears, *Some American Primitives: A Study of New England Faces and Folk Portraits*, Boston, 1941, pl. 64.

22:40a Lewis Mumford, *The Brown Decades*, New York, 1931, pp. 96-106.

21:36b Worthington Whittredge, 'Autobiography,' ed. by J. I. H. Baur, *Brooklyn Museum Journal*, I, 1942, p. 54.

22:31b François Millet, 'Pears,' Boston Museum of Fine Arts. Vincent van Gogh, 'The Apples,' 1887, Austin, op. cit. *The Painters . . .* , no. 15 of the catalogue.

22:36b Montenegro, op. cit. pl. 58.

22:53b Fanny H. Eckstrom, 'Old Time New England,' *Bulletin of the Society for the Preservation of New England Antiquities*, III, 1939, no. 2, p. 65.

Annie Hardy (1839-1934), a daughter of Jeremiah P. Hardy, was her father's pupil and painted charming flower pieces in the eighteen-eighties. They are honest and in all their attention to detail full of authentic feeling. Old photographs of some of them were made accessible to me through Miss Charlotte W. Hardy, Brewer, Maine, but they were not clear enough to be reproduced. Annie Hardy later on, under the influence of Abbott Thayer, changed her style. To judge from a photograph of one of her flower pieces in the L. D. M. Sweat Memorial Art Museum, Portland, Maine, the broad and fluent technique that she acquired from Thayer was not well suited to express her subtle, tender, and unassuming attitude toward nature. An exhibition of her work was held at the Bangor Society of Art, Bangor, Maine, after her death and was reviewed in the *Daily News* of Bangor.

23:3a Photograph in the possession of Miss Charlotte W. Hardy, in Brewer, Maine.

23:18a Bartlett Cowdrey and Hermann Warner Williams, Jr., *William Sidney Mount*, New York, 1944, p. 28.

23:27b Frank Jewett Mather, Jr., 'American Paintings at Princeton University,' *Record of the Museum of Historic Art, Princeton University*, II, 1943, no. 2, p. 6.

24:1a Edgar Preston Richardson, *American Romantic Painting*, New York, 1944, no. 122.

25:10b Mrs. Frederick K. Lundy, Williamsport, Penn., has kindly put the results of her research at my disposal. Her information, complemented by notes on the back of photographs of Roesen's paintings in the Frick Art Reference Library, is the basis of my discussion of the artist.

V: THE STYLE OF TROMPE L'ŒIL

27:36b Richardson, op. cit. *American . . .* , p. 40.

28:47a After his training as a cadet at West Point was terminated by a duel, Bruff traveled for three years as a crew member of a merchant ship, and finally settled down as a draftsman in the Bureau of Topographical Engineers. In 1849 he organized an expedition to California in the hope of making a fortune in the newly discovered gold fields. His hope did not materialize; he returned in 1851 to Washington. From 1853 to 1869 he was a draftsman in the architect's office of the Treasury Department. In 1876 he was appointed to the office of supervisors at the same department, where he worked almost until his death. Bruff, according to his own statement, designed architectural details, naval equipment, insignia, and many other things for the Government. This material has not yet been examined. Only the sketches from his expedition were published. They are of a more documentary than artistic interest. Little information about Bruff as an artist can be gathered from his posthumous notes, except that he undertook to draw a panorama for a panorama company in Sacramento that approached him in 1851. Cf. Georgia Willis Read and Ruth Gaines, *Gold Rush, The Journals, Drawings, and other Papers of J. Goldsborough Bruff, Captain, Washington City and California Mining Association, April 2, 1849 to July 20, 1851*, with a foreword by F. W. Hodge, New York, 1944. Biography: pp. xxxii-xliv. About the panorama, see pp. 941, 1000, 1001. The section of a panorama of Acapulco, Mexico, is illustrated opposite p. 972.

29:14a A. T. Garner, 'Scientific Sources of the Full Length Landscape: 1850,' *Bulletin of the Metropolitan Museum of Art*, IV, 1945, pp. 59-65.

29:17a Elizabeth McCausland, 'Martin Johnson Heade, 1819-1904,' *Panorama, Harry Shaw Newman Gallery*, I, 1945, no. 1, pp. 4-8.

30:12b Edith Gregor Halpert, *'Nature Vive' by William M. Harnett* (exhibition catalogue), Downtown Gallery, New York, 1939. Edward Alden Jewell, 'Works by Harnett Put on Exhibition,' *The New York Times*, 19 April 1939. 'More Recognition for Harnett,' *Antiques*, XLI, 1942, pp. 199-200. H. W. Williams, 'Notes on William M. Harnett,' *Antiques*, XLIII, 1943, pp. 260-62.

31:11a G. D. Davisson, *California Palace of the Legion of Honor Bulletin*, I, 1943, pp. 65-8.

31:15b E. Taylor Snow, 'William M. Harnett,' *American Catholic Researches*, x, 1893, pp. 74-6 (with a photograph of the artist).

31:31b The odd character of *Raspberries and Ice Cream* has aroused suspicion about its authenticity—doubts that do not seem to be warranted, however.

32:36b Apart from Peck, King, and Bruff, the miniature painter Charles Fraser (Charleston, S. C., 1782-1860) painted some still lifes in the style of *trompe l'œil*. One, *Cat Looking at Game*, is, according to the Frick Art Reference Library, in the possession of Theodore H. Willer, Charleston, S. C. The other one, *Game*, is, according to the same source, in the collection of Mrs. Henry Conner, also of Charleston. Photographs of both pictures are in the Frick Art Reference Library.

33:38a J. O'Connor, Jr., 'The Trophy of the Hunt,' *Carnegie Magazine*, XV, 1942, pp. 245-8.

33:49a Barbara Neville and N. Parker, 'Old Cupboard by W. M. Harnett,' *Bulletin of the Museum of Fine Arts*, Boston, XXXVII, 1940, pp. 17-18.

33:47b Edouard Roditi, 'William Harnett, American Necromantic,' *View*, series V, no. 4, pp. 9, 19, 320.

34:12a 'Notes,' *Bulletin of the Metropolitan Museum of Art*, New York, XXXV, 1940, pp. 134-5.

34:14b Arthur Everett Austin, Jr., *Twenty-Five American Paintings from the Revolution to the Civil War*, foreword of a catalogue (n.d., n.p.), p. 5.

34:25b 'Springfield: Nineteenth Century U. S. Still Life,' *Art News*, XXXVII, 1939, no. 1, p. 13.

35:18a 'Discarded Treasures by William Harnett,' *Collection of Art*, Northampton, Mass., 1939, no. 20, pp. 7-18.

35:40b Maude Kemper Riley, 'This Matter of Forgery,' *M.K.R.'s Art Outlook*, Feb. 1946, no. 7, pp. 6-7. Reprint from *Ocean County Courier* (Island Heights, N. Y., published in 1939):

'In many homes in this section today you might find some of his canvases, chiefly small bits of still life. Mr. Peto's studio at Island Heights is today just as he left it when he died. He built it fifty years ago, and from time to time placed this article and that, and his wife has preserved it faithfully. The large fireplace is there in the room with its high, slanting, double ceilings. Innumerable antiques lure the eye. Mr. Peto's easel stands as he left it with his jug of brushes close by. On the walls some of the works of his own creation are seen, with a number of canvases of contemporary artists. These brother painters made a rendezvous of John Frederick's Island Heights studio. John Frederick Peto was one of the early active members of the Art Club of Philadelphia and exhibited annually in the Academy of Fine Arts in the Quaker City.'

36:30a 'Obituary,' *Art News*, 17 Dec. 1910.
36:31b According to information from Director Frederick R. Robinson, the painting once decorated a bar room.
36:34b Miss Nora E. Cordingley of Harvard College Library traced the lost picture.
36:51b *Selections from the correspondence of Theodore Roosevelt and Henry Cabot Lodge*, 1884-1918, New York, 1925, I, pp. 102-4. A quotation from a letter dated 4 Oct. 1890 gives a vivid picture of Theodore Roosevelt's life at Elkhorn Ranch: 'Bay is in excellent health, hardy and stout, I think I may say he is enjoying himself thoroughly. He has recently killed a blacktail doe, and a number of ducks, and was up all night with us fighting a prairie fire—a less simple operation than it sounds. We shall start home about a week hence.'
37:18a Hovard L. Cave, 'Alexander Pope, Painter of Animals,' *Brush and Pencil*, VIII, 1901, pp. 105-12.

VI: FROM NATURALISM TO ROMANTICISM

38:6a Frederick A. Sweet, *The Hudson River School and the Early American Landscape Tradition* (catalogue), The Art Institute of Chicago, 1945.
38:14a Germain Bapst, *Essai sur l'histoire des panoramas et des dioramas*, Paris, 1891. D. Coke, op. cit. ch. v. W. Telbin, 'The Painting of Panoramas,' *Magazine of Art*, XXVI, 1900, pp. 535-58.
38:25a Franz Maria Feldhaus, in *Die Technik der Vorzeit, der geschichtlichen Zeit und der Naturvölker*, Leipzig, 1914, under the heading 'Panorama' mentions the Pleorama, a strip of pictures passing in front of the spectator. This contraption arouses the illusion of moving in the spectator. It was used for the representation of river scenery in 1832 by K. F. Langhaus in Berlin. The Mississippi Panorama was possibly derived from the Pleorama. J. R. Smith, *Descriptive Book of the Tour of Europe, The Largest Moving Panorama, now exhibiting at the Chinese Room, Broadway, New York*, New York, 1853, p. 3. J. F. Mc-

Dermott, 'Newsreel—Old Style,' *Antiques*, XLIV, 1943, pp. 10-13.
38:28a Wolfgang Born, 'Sources of American Romanticism,' *Antiques*, XLVIII, 1945, pp. 274-7.
39:52a Harry T. Peters, *Currier and Ives*, New York, 1926, I, pp. 110-16.
40:3a Henry Pleasants, Jr., *250 Years of Painting in Maryland* (catalogue), The Baltimore Museum of Art, 1945, nos. 154, 155.
41:5a Royal Cortissoz, *John La Farge: A Memoir and a Study*, Boston, 1911, p. 116.
41:9b Frederick Fairchild Sherman, 'Some Early Oil Paintings by John La Farge,' *Art in America*, VIII, 1920, pp. 85-91.
42:14b Guy Pène du Bois, *William Glackens*, Whitney Museum of American Art, New York, 1932.
42:35b Mr. Denis L. Peterkin of Andover, Mass. put at my disposal the biographical notes that were used for my discussion of the artist, whose name was first mentioned to me by Mr. Lionello Venturi. It was only after the manuscript went to press that the catalogues of the exhibition held first in Andover and afterwards in New York became known to me. See: Addison Gallery of American Art, Phillips Academy, Andover, Mass., 'Arthur Clifton Goodwin: A Selective Exhibition,' 1946; and Wildenstein (gallery), New York, 'An Exhibition of Oils and Pastels by Arthur C. Goodwin,' 1946 (with contributions by Denis L. Peterkin [The Man] and by Lionello Venturi [The Artist]).

VII: THE GROWTH OF PRECISIONISM

44:9a Margaret Breuning, *Maurice Prendergast*, American Art Series, Whitney Museum of American Art, New York, 1931.
44:4b George Biddle, *Adolphe Borie*, Washington, 1937.
44:34b Oscar Hagen, *The Birth of the American Tradition in Art*, New York, 1940.
45:15a Peter H. Brieger, 'Baroque Equation: Illusion and Reality,' *Gazette des Beaux-Arts*, 6th series, XXXVII, 1945, pp. 143-64.
45:16b Murray, David, *Museums: Their History and Their Use.* With a bibliography and list of museums in the United Kingdom, Glasgow, 1904, I, p. 179f.
45:30b Georgia O'Keeffe's symbolistic paintings of bones and flowers show a certain affinity to the Precisionist style, but they recall modern decorative art rather than photography and cubism.
46:1a A. E. Gallatin, *Charles Demuth*, New York, 1927. William Murrell, *Charles Demuth*, American Art Series, Whitney Museum of American Art, New York (n.d.), XVII.
46:41a 'Preston Dickinson, 1891-1930, Exhibition, Knoedler Galleries, February 15th,' *Art Digest*, 15 Feb. 1943, p. 12.
47:14a Constance Rourke, *Charles Sheeler, Artist in the American Tradition*, New York, 1938.

PLATES

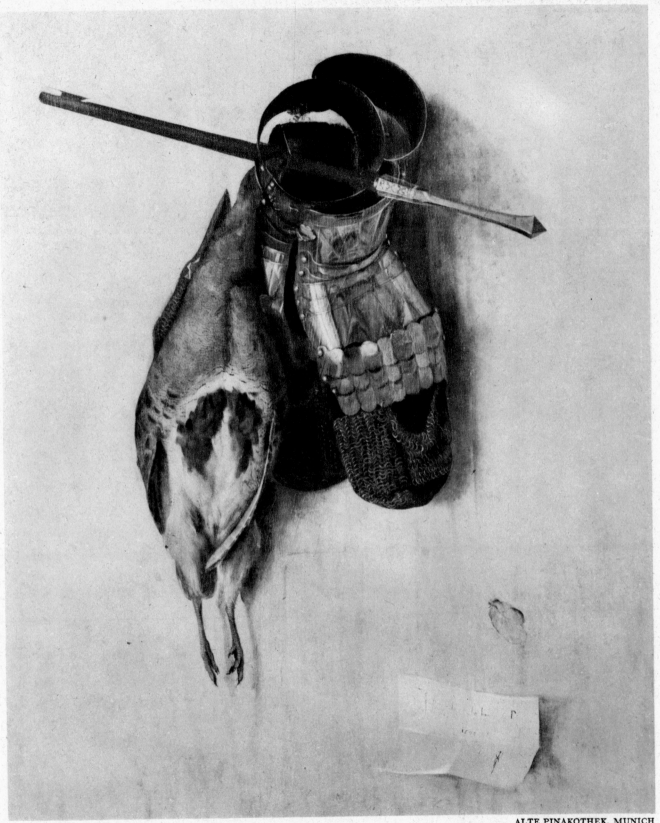

1. *Dead Partridge* BY JACOPO DE BARBARI

2. *The Dead Cock* BY MELCHIOR DE HONDECOETER

3. *Letter Rack* by WALLERANT VAILLANT

4. *Perspective Box of a Dutch Interior with Still Life* by Samuel van Hoogstraten

NEW-YORK HISTORICAL SOCIETY

5. *Close-up of Underbrush with Animals* BY OTTO MARSAEUS VAN SCHRIECK

6. *Library* BY JEAN-BAPTISTE OUDRY

7. *Still Life* BY APPOLINAR FONSECA

8. *Still Life* BY FRANCISCO DE ZURBARAN

9. *Still Life* BY CARAVAGGIO

10. *Kitchen Still Life* BY JEAN-BAPTISTE SIMEON CHARDIN

11. *Flowers* BY CORNELIUS VAN SPAENDONCK

12. *Still Life, Fruit and Flowers* BY FRANZ XAVER PETTER

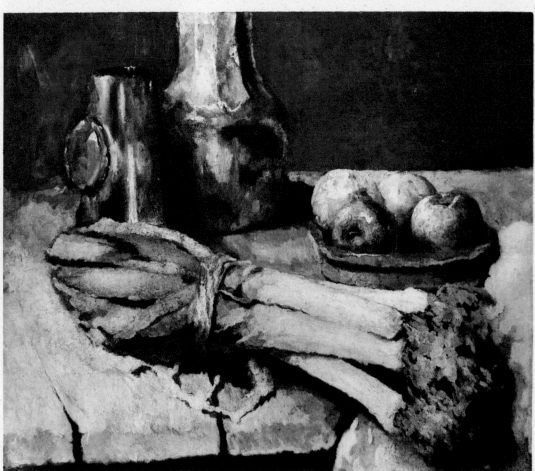

13. *Still Life* BY CARL SCHUCH

14. *Fruit Bowl, Detail of Family Group* BY CHARLES WILLSON PEALE

15. *Fruits of Autumn* BY JAMES PEALE

16. *Still Life, Fruit* BY JAMES PEALE

17. *Still Life, Fruit* BY JAMES PEALE

18. *Still Life, Watermelon and Grapes* BY JAMES PEALE

19. *Apples and Fox Grapes* BY RAPHAELLE PEALE

20. *Still Life with a Glass, Plate, Biscuit and Fruit* BY RAPHAELLE PEALE

21. *Still Life with Peaches* BY RAPHAELLE PEALE

22. *Still Life with Watermelon* BY RAPHAELLE PEALE

23. *Still Life with Wild Strawberries* BY RAPHAELLE PEALE

24. *Still Life, Liqueur and Fruit* BY RAPHAELLE PEALE

25. *Still Life with Vegetables* BY RAPHAELLE PEALE

26. *Still Life, Melons* BY RAPHAELLE PEALE

27. *Fruit in Basket* BY ROBERT STREET

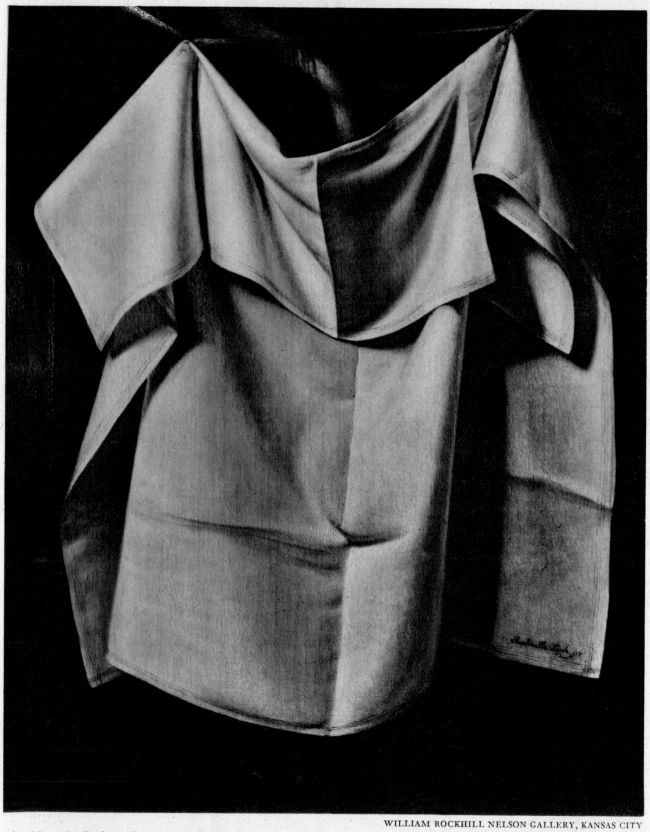

28. *After the Bath* BY RAPHAELLE PEALE

29. *Peaches* BY SARAH PEALE

30. *Still Life with Fruit in a Bowl* ATTRIBUTED TO JAMES PEALE

31. *Still Life* ARTIST UNKNOWN

32. *Flower Piece* BY RUBENS PEALE

33. *Two Grouse in Underbrush of Laurel* BY RUBENS PEALE

34. *The American Dessert* BY RUBENS PEALE

35. *Bowl with Apples* BY ABRAHAM WOODSIDE

36. Strawberries and Cherries BY MARGARETTA ANGELICA PEALE

37. Still Life with Apples and Watermelons BY GEORGE COPE

38. *Spring Flowers in Vase* BY MARY JANE PEALE

39. *Stylized Flowers* PENNSYLVANIA GERMAN FOLK ART

40. *Assorted Fruit* ARTIST UNKNOWN

41. *Still Life with Melons and Grapes* BY CHIPMAN

42. *Basket of Flowers and Fruit* BY ADELE EVANS

43. *Still Life with Singing Bird* ARTIST UNKNOWN

44. *Flower Basket and Fruits* BY AMORY L. BABCOCK

45. *Flowers on Black Marble Table* ARTIST UNKNOWN

46. *Blue Urn with Peonies and Roses* ARTIST UNKNOWN

47. *Mrs. Boyd and Mrs. Smith* BY THOMAS SULLY

48. *Fruit* ARTIST UNKNOWN

MARY VINCENT.

49. *Tipped Bowl* BY MARY VINCENT

50. *Basket of Fruit* ARTIST UNKNOWN

51. *Basket of Fruit* ARTIST UNKNOWN

52. *Spring Bouquet* BY WILLIAM S. MOUNT

53. *Déjeuner à la Fourchette* BY JOSEPH BIAYS ORD

54. *Grapes in a Dish* BY JOHN F. FRANCIS

55. *Cheese, Chestnuts, and Crackers* BY JOHN F. FRANCIS

56. *Apples in a Basket* BY JOHN F. FRANCIS

57. *Still Life with Biscuit* BY JOHN F. FRANCIS

58. *Still Life with Upturned Cherry Basket* BY JOHN F. FRANCIS

59. *Still Life with Raisins and Oranges* BY JOHN F. FRANCIS

60. *Still Life* BY JOHN F. FRANCIS

61. *Three Pears Between Grapes* BY G. P. HARDY

62. *Nature's Bounty* BY SEVERIN ROESEN

63. *Flowers* BY SEVERIN ROESEN

64. *Fruits* BY SEVERIN ROESEN

65. *The Wedding Gifts* BY JAMES WELLES CHAMPNEY

66. *Holly* BY GEORGE H. HALL

67. *The All-Seeing Eye* BY NATHANIEL PECK

68. *Time Is Money* BY F. DANTON, JR. (Reproduced by special permission of the Secretary of the Treasury)

69. *Vanity of an Artist's Dream* BY CHARLES BIRD KING

70. Assorted Prints by Goldsborough Bruff

71. *Flower Still Life* BY MARTIN J. HEADE

72. *Orchids and Hummingbird* BY MARTIN J. HEADE

73. *Gremlin in the Studio* BY MARTIN J. HEADE

74. *Still Life* BY MORSTON CONSTANTINE REAM

JOHN JACOB ASTOR, NEW YORK

75. Locomotive Entering Yard at Night ARTIST UNKNOWN

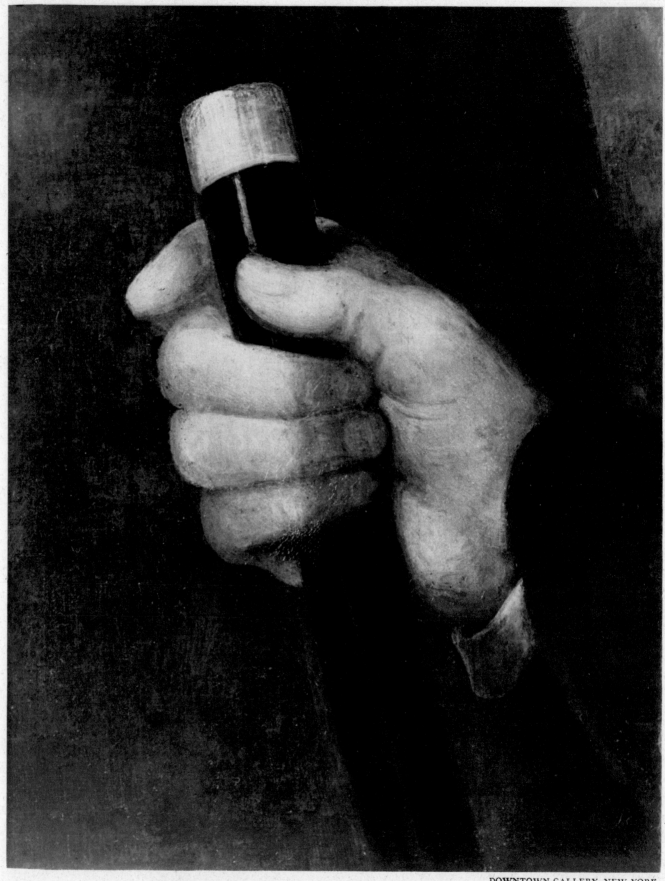

76. *To the Opera* BY WILLIAM M. HARNETT

77. *Raspberries and Ice Cream* BY WILLIAM M. HARNETT

78. Writing Table BY WILLIAM M. HARNETT

79. Basket of Catawba Grapes BY WILLIAM M. HARNETT

80. *Just Dessert* BY WILLIAM M. HARNETT

81. *Still Life with New York Ledger* BY WILLIAM M. HARNETT

82. *Fruit Piece* BY WILLIAM M. HARNETT

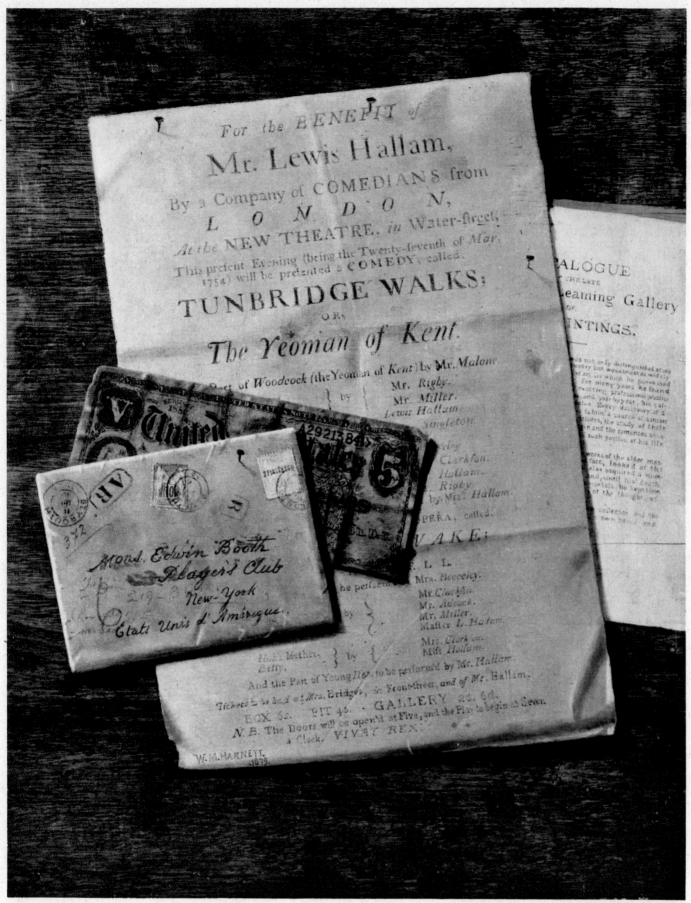

83. *To Edwin Booth* BY WILLIAM M. HARNETT

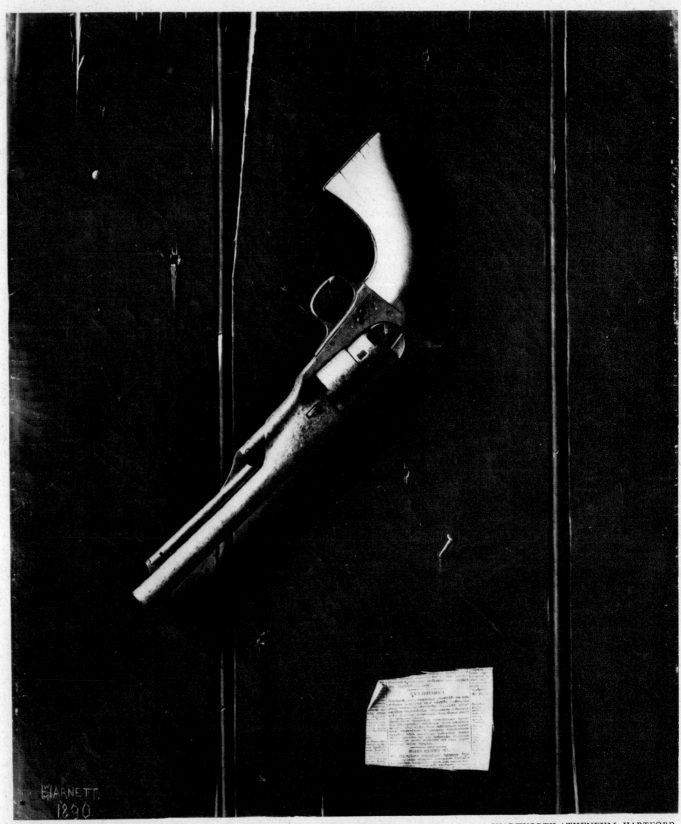

84. *The Faithful Colt* BY WILLIAM M. HARNETT

85. *Old Souvenirs* BY WILLIAM M. HARNETT

86. *For Sunday Dinner* BY WILLIAM M. HARNETT

87. *The Trophy of the Hunt* BY WILLIAM M. HARNETT

88. *Mandolin* BY WILLIAM M. HARNETT

89 The Old Cupboard Door BY WILLIAM M. HARNETT

90. *Discarded Treasures* BY WILLIAM M. HARNETT

91. *Ten-Cent Bill* BY WILLIAM M. HARNETT (Reproduced by special permission of the Secretary of the Treasury)

92. *Time, Religion and Politics* BY W. S. REYNOLDS

93. *Twenty-Dollar Bill* BY J. HABERLE (Reproduced by special permission of the Secretary of the Treasury)

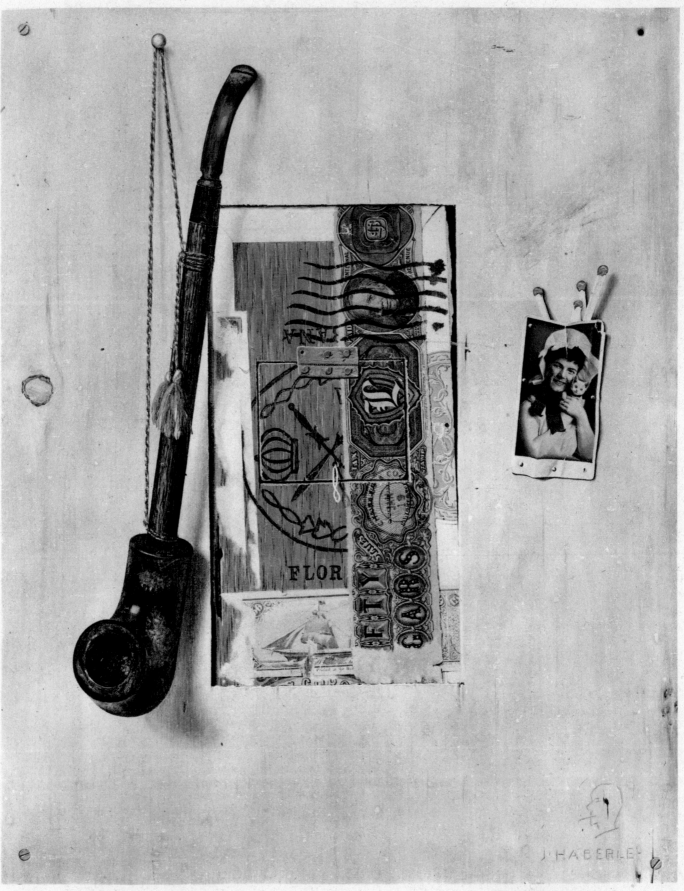

94. *Cigar Box and Pipe* BY J. HABERLE

95. Memories of 1865 BY JOHN F. PETO

96. Theodore Roosevelt's Cabin Door BY RICHARD LaBARRE GOODWIN

97. Woodcock BY EDMUND E. CASE

98. *Quail* BY ALEXANDER POPE

99. *Landscape, Fruit and Flowers* BY FRANCES PALMER (BOND)

100. *Apples* BY A. J. H. WAY

101. *Still Life with Flagon and Fruits* BY EDWARD BOWERS

102. *Flower Piece* BY RALPH ALBERT BLAKELOCK

103. *Laurel Blossoms in a Blue Vase* BY WORTHINGTON WHITTREDGE

104. *Hollyhocks* ARTIST UNKNOWN

105. *Still Life with Watermelon* BY FRANK DUVENECK

106. *Calla Lily* BY JOHN LA FARGE

107. *Magnolia Grandiflora* BY JOHN LA FARGE

108. *Hollyhocks and Corn* BY JOHN LA FARGE

109. *Vase of Flowers* BY JOHN LA FARGE

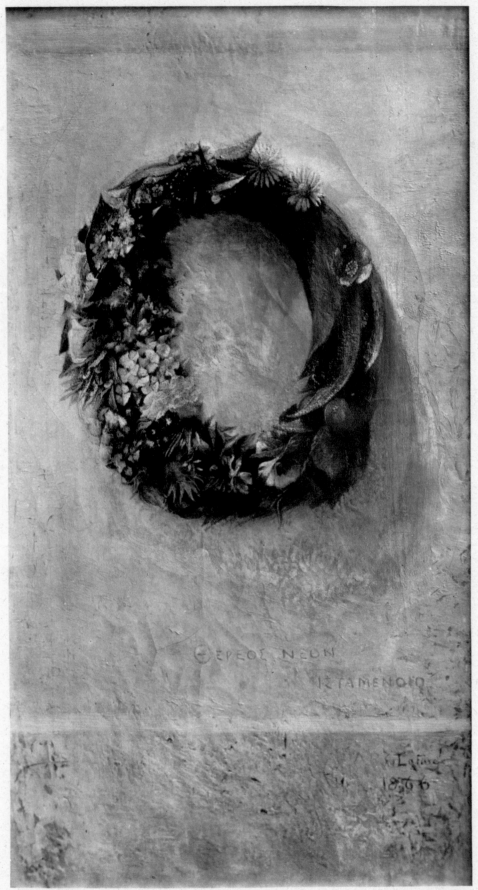

110. *Wreath* BY JOHN LA FARGE

111. *An English Cod* BY WILLIAM MERRITT CHASE

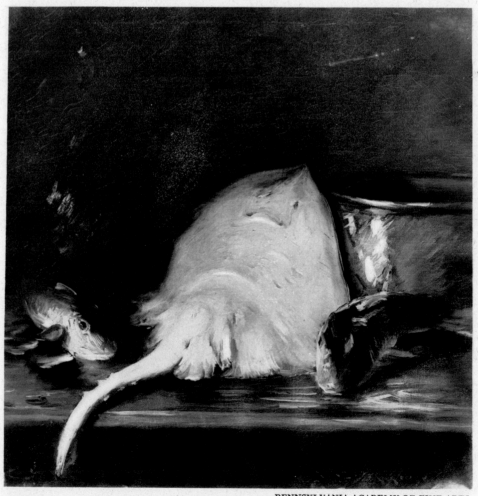

112. *Still Life with Fish* BY WILLIAM MERRITT CHASE

113. *The White Jug* BY EMIL CARLSEN

114. *Still Life* BY EMIL CARLSEN

115. *The Delft Plate* BY J. ALDEN WEIR

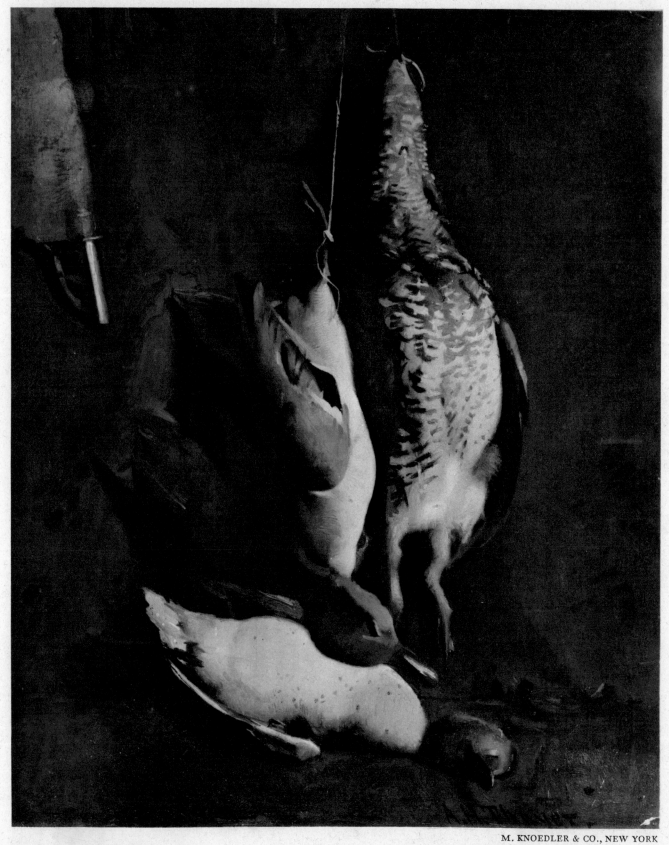

116. *Still Life* BY A. H. THAYER

117. *Still Life* BY L. KOECHLIN

118. *Alpine Field Flowers* BY FREDERICK C. FRIESECKE

119. *Apples* BY CHILDE HASSAM

120. *Flowers in a Sugar Bowl* BY WILLIAM GLACKENS

121. *Flowers* by Arthur Clifton Goodwin

122. *Vase of Flowers* BY MAURICE PRENDERGAST

123. *Stone Fruit* BY ADOLPHE BORIE

124. *Eggplant and Squash* BY CHARLES DEMUTH

125. *Daisies* BY CHARLES DEMUTH

126. *Red and Yellow Gladioli* BY CHARLES DEMUTH

127. *Still Life, Flowers* BY PRESTON DICKINSON

128. *Hospitality* BY PRESTON DICKINSON

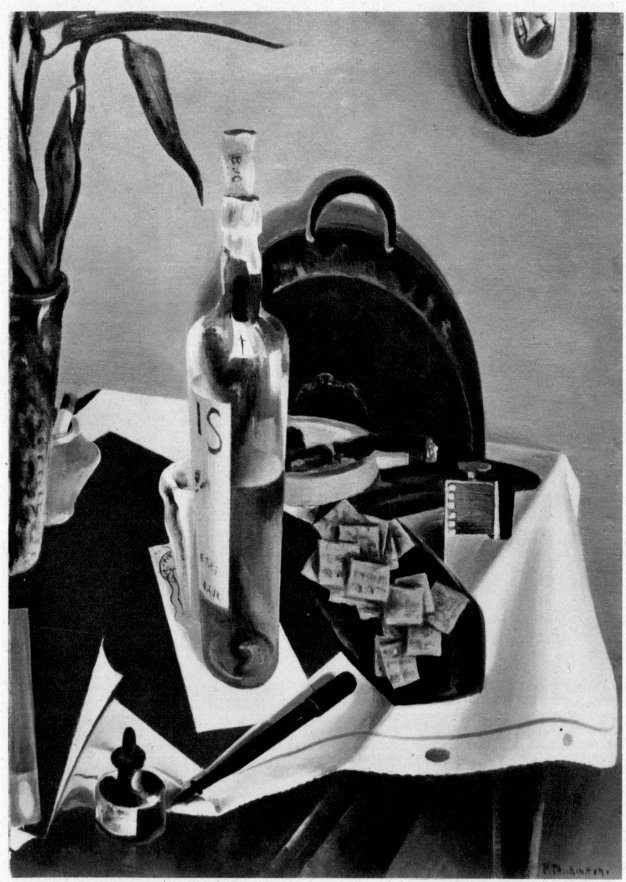

129. *Still Life with Bottle* BY PRESTON DICKINSON

WALTER C. ARENSBERG, HOLLYWOOD, CAL.

130. *Cactus* by Charles Sheeler

131. *Still Life with Teapot* BY CHARLES SHEELER

132. *Spring Interior* BY CHARLES SHEELER

133. *Boneyard* BY CHARLES SHEELER

134. *Rolling Power* BY CHARLES SHEELER